sex
TALK

**how to tell
your lover
exactly what
you want,
exactly when
you want it**

SOURCEBOOKS CASABLANCA™
AN IMPRINT OF SOURCEBOOKS, INC.®
NAPERVILLE, ILLINOIS

CAROLE ALTMAN, PhD

Published by Sourcebooks, Inc.
P.O. Box 4410, Naperville, Illinois 60567-4410
(630) 961-3900
FAX: (630) 961-2168
www.sourcebooks.com

Library of Congress Cataloging-in-Publication Data

Altman, Carole.
  Sex talk : how to tell your lover exactly what you want, exactly when you
want it / Carole Altman.
     p. cm.
  ISBN 1-4022-0301-2 (alk. paper)
 1. Sex. 2. Sex instruction. 3. Interpersonal communication. 4. Intimacy
(Psychology) I. Title.

HQ31.A49392 2004
613.9'6—dc22

                         2004016835

                  Printed and bound in Canada
                  TR 10 9 8 7 6 5 4 3 2 1

To my daughter Jodi Amosuro and my grandchildren Robbie and Alyssa because they have truly learned that love is the energy of life and that generosity is the golden prize of the rainbow.

Acknowledgments

I deeply appreciate and respect the men and women who invited me into their bedrooms and into their hearts, helping me to write *Sex Talk*.

Thanks to my editor Deb Werksman, whose literary skills enhance my every word, and to my agent Sheree Bykofsky, who had unparalleled faith in me. Special thanks to Megan Buckley, whose help has been invaluable.

My many brilliant friends and colleagues who offered their expertise, love, and support are also very much appreciated. Dr. Ruthellen Rosenfelder, Dr. Chuck Miller, Dr. Freyda Zell, Jodi Amoruso, Karen Rose, Betty Tobon, Nikki Hyson, Joan Gassman, Claire McGraw, and Gila Michael. These wonderful friends shared their time and knowledge with sweet generosity. Thank you to Robbie and Alyssa Amoruso because I am constantly energized and enthralled with my life because of my love for them.

I am especially appreciative and grateful to the loving and positive Spirits which guide me.

Table of Contents

preface

Sex Talk offers you ideas and concepts to use in your pursuit of pleasure. *Sex Talk* is a guideline for developing thriving lines of communication for a more honest and successful relationship. *Sex Talk* is a compilation of techniques and practices that inform and demonstrate how to experience the ecstasy of electrifying sex. It is your manifesto to open, gratifying, and successful intimate discussions. *Sex Talk* details the secrets to developing and perpetuating respect and desire for more loving and joyous connections.

Sex Talk is a key to unlocking the attitudes and emotions that allow certain sexual pleasures, yet restrict others. These methods open doors to visions of unique, unfamiliar, and spectacular sexuality that may have gone unexplored.

Sex Talk offers not only ideas and concepts, but methods, techniques, contracts, and questionnaires that enable you to experience positive results.

Sex Talk addresses the issue of continuing old patterns and behaviors that have seemed sufficiently satisfying, yet leave a sense of dissatisfaction and frustration. Despite the dissatisfaction level of certain sexual techniques, these behaviors continue to be the choice of many, since we seem to choose the "easy way." Many men feel that the very common missionary position is the easiest and most intimate form of sexual intercourse. Yet, women do not achieve enough clitoral stimulation in this position. *Sex Talk* encourages, describes, and motivates so that you learn the most satisfying techniques, and become more creative and experimental to enhance pleasure.

Sex Talk encourages you to look into the wide array of experiences that may be more fulfilling and more exciting. *Sex Talk* recognizes that always taking the easy way may cause disappointment and frustration, and create pain and suffering because of boredom and anger.

Sex Talk opens the possibility that you may be maintaining the status quo and avoiding any questions or dissatisfactions that you have. Avoidance allows us to accept what we have and not struggle for more, even if we feel frustration and disappointment, even if we would love to have more. *Sex Talk* addresses this with down-to-earth, real solutions that actually work and have been successful for thousands of people.

Because it is clear that taking the easy way out often deprives you of the pleasures that are available, and to which you are certainly entitled, *Sex Talk* encourages you to look beyond, to take risks, to involve yourself in the wonders of the unknown. Enhanced pleasure can be yours by following the ideas and techniques detailed in *Sex Talk*.

Often your pleasure center is obstructed or avoided because of inhibitions, judgmental attitudes, or fears of unpleasant consequences. *Sex Talk* observes these tendencies and offers ideas that help to overcome any barriers that diminish feelings or limit satisfaction. Throughout the book, you encounter questionnaires and contracts to help you to clarify and solidify your ideas, beliefs, and attitudes. These are offered to help you gain greater awareness and determination.

Questionnaires provoke the imagination and open your mind to thoughts and fantasies which you've been unwilling to verbalize or even consider. The responses to questionnaires create the links of shared information so that each of you is aware of your needs and wants. Often it is embarrassing or even impossible for us to share certain desires. However, when responding to a question, it becomes possible. Questionnaires are your road to complete openness and increased pleasures.

When you discover feelings and fantasies you want to make real, you can use the tools of *Sex Talk* to make them real, to give yourself more pleasure, and to create an atmosphere of freedom and connection between your partner and yourself. These questionnaires allow you to discuss, share, and bring new behaviors to your relationship, thereby satisfying many of your needs; needs which may have been hidden and ignored. Employing these tools will deepen your creativity as a partner in sex, and especially intensify your pleasure for and with each other.

Remember, you are very likely to build resentment and anger if you are not sexually fulfilled. It is actually unfair to blame your lover if you have not done your part in asking and otherwise making known what it is that pleases you.

Sex Talk enables you to not only share your sexual and emotional needs, but to recognize for yourself what these needs are. By examining your own body, knowing what you like about kissing, about penetration, about touching, or about sucking, you can share what you've discovered. By listening to your own sounds, recognizing the sounds that turn you on, and learning the sounds that turn on your partner, you enhance and intensify your sexual pleasures.

Sex Talk indicates various situations in which you find yourself frustrated or unfulfilled. You learn to avoid and obliterate such situations, not tolerate them, and be completely free of these moments. How horrible it is to repeat a touch, or a kiss, or a motion that annoys, pains, and frustrates you. Yet many couples actually experience such moments each and every time they make love. The result is that they make love much less often, they begin to move apart, and they eventually separate completely. *Sex Talk* opens your mind and your self-confidence so that you not only become aware of the frustrating situations, but you are also able to talk to your partner, let her know what annoys you, let him know what you need, avoid the irritating behaviors, and replace them with the loving and tenderness you deserve.

Sex Talk teaches how to share your needs during a quiet sharing of responses to questions so that the frustrating behavior is not repeated. *Sex Talk* helps you to create an atmosphere of loving attention, with respect for each other, so that information shared is accepted and not seen as criticism or anger.

If you tell your partner that being touched on your waist tickles, and tickling is a turn-off for you, he will be aware of your needs and not touch your waist during your lustful moments. If you need to be kissed during intercourse, sharing this information will enable you to use only those positions that allow the kissing to continue. If you need more pressure on your penis or clitoris in order to climax, you need to share this as well. Instructing, demanding, or complaining during the heat of passion is not the answer, yet many of us continue to hurt each other in this way. We restrict our pleasures and we create barriers to respect and love. *Sex Talk* is a guide to successfully sharing *all* information, however sensitive, because the sharing is with respect and love, in the proper time and place, and with the most warm and kind approach.

Since it is also true that we do need to stop a certain behavior, or change a position, or ask for more of a particular motion or touch, *Sex Talk* guides you to a style which permits this communication without breaking the tone of the moment. A slight move of the hand, a small turn of the hip, or a long kiss to distract are just some of the ideas we offer for just such situations. *Sex Talk* addresses this issue with many ideas and techniques that will enable you to stop the irritating or frustrating behavior, yet continue with the passion without breaking the rhythm.

How often have you been lustfully writhing, hips thrusting, breathing heavy, body sweating, and suddenly the touch is wrong, or the movement stops? How frustrating has that been? *Sex Talk* shows that you need never suffer such a moment again. You will know how to share your exact needs, at the moment in which you need to.

Sex Talk recognizes the need to reward and recognize so that positive behavior is encouraged and stimulated. When all is going beautifully, you owe it to yourself and your partner to acknowledge your pleasures, to reward the positive with your words, your sounds, and in other ways that please you both.

Similarly, in *Sex Talk* you are reminded that negative criticism is destructive and demeaning. It will accomplish only separateness and anger, and will certainly not bring you the love and pleasure you crave. Negative criticism creates self-consciousness, discomfort, and possibly even anger.

If your partner is trying to please you, even if it is not totally what you want or need, be grateful and recognize the attempt. Support for all efforts will encourage, but negativity will discourage. Remember the three Rs: Respect, Reward, and Response-Ability. If you maintain these positive feelings when you ask for something, you will be much more likely to achieve your goals, so choose your path, the path of *Sex Talk*, the path of love.

Sex Talk questionnaires can help you to see if and when you struggle with urges to be critical, and how to be positive and complimentary. There are contracts that will help you both to maintain the three Rs and to maintain the love and affection you felt for each other the day you met, or became engaged, or married. Contracts in *Sex Talk* help you to communicate your feelings and your needs, and remind you of how satisfying and fabulous and loving you are to each other, and how good that feels.

The tools provided here are especially useful in helping you appreciate the importance of knowing yourself as a sexual being; knowing what you want, how your body responds to various techniques and touches, and generally what gives you the greatest joy and pleasure consistently. This is the first step to being able to communicate well to your lover. We explore how to share our sexual awareness in a loving, honest, non-threatening way, using words and nonverbal communication. *Sex Talk* takes you on a journey of your sexual behaviors, examining every aspect of the various parts of sex, from kissing to touching to sucking to penetration. With the self-knowledge you discover, you will be able to share your needs by using the tools provided in *Sex Talk*.

Of course, your emotions are an integral part of both your need for and experience of physical sexuality. Throughout the book, techniques and ideas are offered to enhance your emotional well-being as well as your physical pleasures.

Questions of sharing emotional needs are explored, with anecdotes depicting issues that are best *not* to share, and those that *must* be shared. Exploring your own deep and private emotional needs by use of questionnaires and anecdotes, you become more aware and more open to your partner. Through open, honest sharing, consensual behavior, and openness to the emotional and sexual needs and expressions of your partner as well as of yourself, your pleasures will be intensified and your loving connections will be solidified.

The sounds we make during sex frequently communicate our emotional state. You are encouraged to examine your sounds and the sexual words or expressions you tend to use with frequency during sex. Do these vocalizations deepen your experience? Are they honest expressions of what you feel? Do they really communicate to your partner what you mean to communicate? Are you inhibited and unable or unwilling to let go and allow the sounds to express your passion? *Sex Talk* enables you to become aware of the importance of sounds and words and the pleasures they provoke.

Another means of communicating sexually and play- fully is through sex games similar to the ones we suggest. Of course you will invent your own variations as you get into the swing of things (if you haven't already). Games bring fun and laughter, or engage your imagination and deepen involvement, intensity, and the passion you are seeking. They take sex and demystify it—something that brings another quality to your love life. Sometimes sex needs to be brought down to earth, so to speak. Remember the joy of rolling down a grassy hill or making angels in the snow? Remember the sense of total abandonment and freedom you felt at those moments? Sex games allow you to recreate such moments, become a child again, let go and be wild and crazy, funny and delightful, delicious and wondrous. Be the playful child and watch yourselves fall in love with each other all over again. Add this new dimension to your sexual pleasures, and watch the passion explode exponentially.

Sex Talk suggests many positive aspects of sex games including the introduction of sexual behaviors that you have been unwilling to suggest. By using the "game" as a covert way of opening a door to oral sex, or costumes, or bondage, you can feel your way to new dimensions of sexuality, and new pleasures you may have avoided.

Closely allied to playing sexual games is the notion of adding fantasy to your sexual experiences. You are urged first and foremost to be respectful of one another's sexual fantasies and fetishes. So long as there is loving mutual consent, feel free to tell stories, use props, costumes, assumed identities and so forth in your sexual play. You never want sex to be automatic and humdrum. Fantasy and play allows you to vary your behavior and your sources of pleasure, making you a more fascinating sexual partner, freer of inhibitions, more passionate, and thereby more fulfilled.

The more creative you are, the more open and free you are, the less likely your relationship will become boring or asexual.

It is certainly true that candles and oils, showering together and writing little poems, calls during the day, and whispered promises are all wonderful and enticing. What else can you add to your sexual lives? What is more unusual, more exotic, more electrifying? Creativity, imagination, fantasy—these are limitless, without boundaries. These hold the key to ecstasy without end, a love which is magical and forever.

Sex Talk brings you into the bedrooms of many couples. You can become the "fly on the wall" and witness the stories of couples who are practicing some of the techniques offered in this book. You are reintroduced to ideas of assertiveness, acceptance, creativity, and compliance as they relate to involvement in very satisfying sexual encounters. You may see yourself in some of these anecdotes, recall how you might have made assertiveness work for you, or how you creatively turned a routine lovemaking into a time of memorable passion. As with just about everything else in life, you get more out of lovemaking if you put more into it! It's really as simple as that. Relationships improve with attention, with determination, with imagination, and with a great deal of effort.

We spend more time on a recipe for dinner than we do on our recipes for love. *Sex Talk* offers many recipes for love, for sex, for communication, and for connection. Use them with love and with caring and you will reap the benefits. A mouth-watering meal, well prepared, memorably delicious, and exciting to the palate is nothing compared to the benefits of a recipe for love.

On that note, you are sent forth with many wonderful tools and the best of wishes for a life full of electrifying sex and enduring love. I feel that love is the energy of life; without it we wither. Maintain the energy of love. Bloom with love every day. Use each moment to enhance and improve your love. Be good to yourself and attain your goals. You deserve the best of love—so do whatever it takes, but get what you deserve.

With Love,
Carole Altman

chapter 1

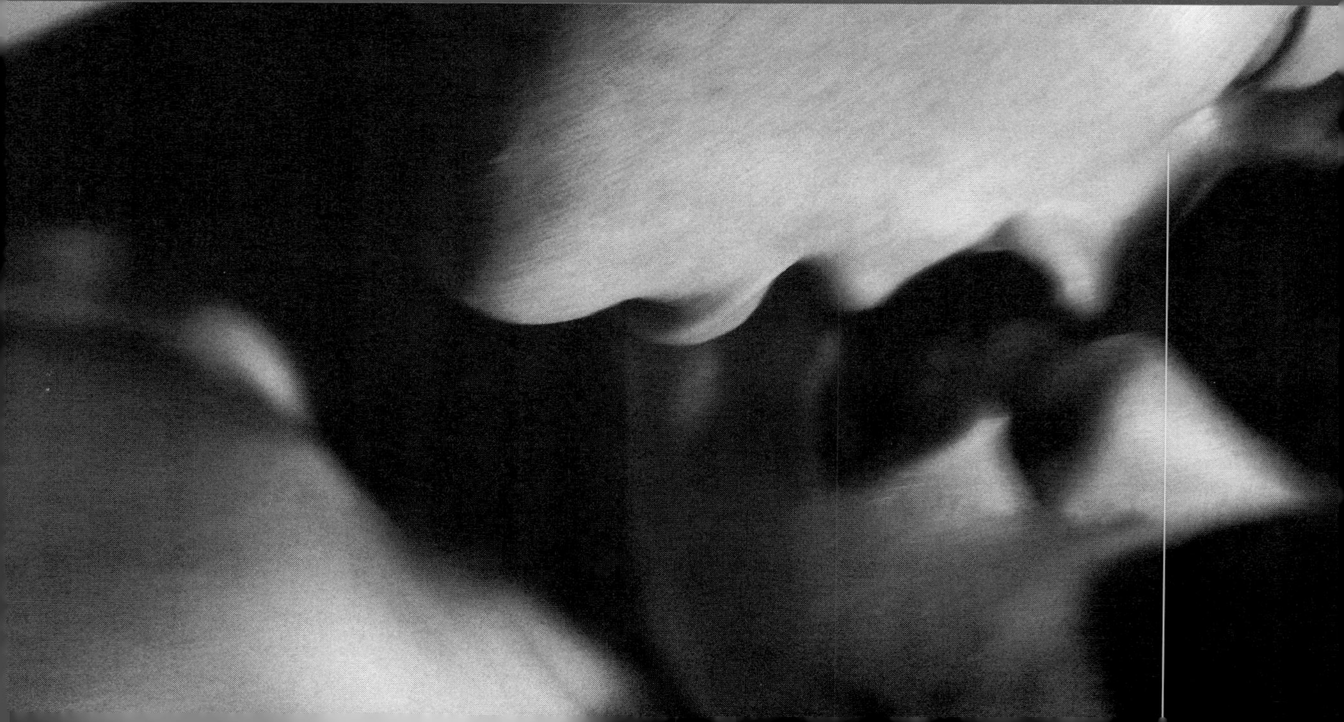

introduction

You can hear your heart it's beating so loudly. Your juices are flowing, your breathing shallow and slow. Your body is arched to meet his, moving rhythmically and deliciously. Your muscles contract so tightly you can feel small spasms throughout your body. You can barely breathe, your body is tightening into itself, drawing you into a tunnel of moaning and purring. You feel yourself on the threshold of another glorious moment of release.

He shifts just slightly. The change in his pace is barely noticeable. However minimal the change, your moment shifts also, downwards and away from that perfect blend of stimulation and love. You wish it were a Woody Allen movie so that a drill sergeant could shout from behind the headboard, "Maintain position and speed, no deviations, soldier."

Why didn't you say, "I love it; don't stop, don't change, don't do anything different." If only you'd said, "This is it, it's perfect, it's as it should be."

You could have told him how exquisite the moment was. It might have been a good idea to tell him not to change anything, his movements, his pace, his position, or his rhythm. Why didn't you say something so that he knew how delicate this moment was? If he knew how precarious your state of passion was, he might not have shifted. Just a word or two might have held this moment in its perfection.

Of course, your lovemaking continues, and your state of passion and moment of release will return. Of course loving is always delicious and wondrous and part of the glory of sexual expression. The big O, however luscious, is not the only reason we love to get naked together. Actually, the orgasm is not even an absolute necessity. In fact I never refer to any lovemaking as foreplay. I call it moreplay. I don't believe that any touching and kissing and hugging and penetrating is before anything. I believe that it is all part of the pleasure we give to each other, and very much a part of our connection to each other.

It is also true that at that special moment when all systems are go, and you are ready for that flight to completion and ecstasy, it is best not to have any interruptions. So why don't we say so? Why not say just a word or two to let your partner know there can be no modifications? Just a word or two would maintain the miracle. Why do we remain silent?

We keep our fantasies, our fetishes, and our special needs a secret. If we were more open and honest we'd not only enjoy more pleasure, we'd enjoy the type of pleasure which is special and unique to us. We don't say that we don't like a certain touch and we rarely say what type of touch we do like. We kiss, but without detailing the intricacies of kissing which are especially delicious.

We ignore our own discomfort or displeasure because we fear insulting or hurting our partner. We neglect to say what we want, how we want it, and when we want it. We allow a special moment to pass rather than intrude on feelings or ego. We actually deprive ourselves in deference to our beliefs that we have to protect our lovers from the humiliation of requests or corrections.

Most of the time our beliefs are unfounded. If we learn how to express ourselves without judgment or anger, we can actually get what we want without unpleasant repercussions. *Sex Talk* is a guide that not only advises and demonstrates, but shares personal successes of men and women who reaped the benefits of telling it like they needed it told, asking for it as they needed it done, and successfully getting it the way they wanted it.

We are treading a fragile path in our attempts to fulfill our intimate sexual dreams and hopes. It's essential that we look at some basic skills to keep in mind as we share our intimate needs. Of course, at the height of the moment, these ideas are somewhat irrelevant. By using this lighthouse of good sharing and bad sharing, our success rate will soar. In addition, as we begin to speak about our sexual needs outside of the bedroom, we will be able to express them more easily and comfortably at the moment.

First, there is a basic truth about the differences between men and women which plays a huge role in the way we hear each other. Our levels of emotional investment in various areas are extremely dissimilar. Women are emotionally invested in being listened to, whereas men are invested in being able to create a solution. Women want to just talk about a problem, whereas men want to do something to fix it. Women need to understand that unless a man feels that he is a hero about an issue, he finds it difficult to listen to her needs or problems. Men need to understand that a woman doesn't need the solution as much as she needs compassion and empathy. If we keep these differences in mind when we begin to share our sex talk, success will be more frequent and disappointment will be avoided.

Another aspect of good sex talk is the when and the how, which is even more important than the what. We've heard the expression, "take it from whom it comes." There is great truth in this statement because regardless of the message, the relevant factor is *who* is sending the message. It is also *how* the message is expressed, which is equally relevant. Another factor is *when* the message is heard. Timing is crucial.

1. Speak with love and respect for your partner. (Who)

2. Be sure that love and respect are first and foremost, above the content of the message. (How)

3. Be sure you have an agreement, either explicit or implicit, to have a conversation. (When)

4. Share feelings and needs, not demands or judgments.

It is also true that *what* we say can be misunderstood. We hear through our own filter system and may interpret the message differently than it was meant. There are many factors in every conversation that, if ignored, can create miscommunication and perhaps disaster.

Consider the above suggestions with recognition of how essential they are. By utilizing these factors at all times, you will insure successful sharing and successful sex talk.

Our emotions are often an invisible umbrella encapsulating and deciphering each expression to meet our own personal needs. Be aware of your own emotions as well as your partner's. Don't tread on sands so soft you're in danger of sinking. Speak when the timing is right. Speak only if there is an agreement to have a serious discussion. These are aspects of being respectful and loving. By following these guidelines, your ground is firm, and your messages more acceptable.

Let's always keep in mind that each of us has a filter system through which we speak and hear. These work in magical ways. Sometimes we "hear" the real message. But often we hear what we "want to hear." Too often we hear a distorted interpretation which supports and encourages our own needs. I've seen and heard thousand of these distortions.

For example, it is difficult for most of us to hear a suggestion or request regarding certain behaviors. We hear it as a negative criticism and we become defensive, even angry.

A friend of mine was furious at his wife because she told him she believed one of his employees was probably stealing. He heard these words as criticism of his management skills and that he was a failure as a businessman. He also thought his wife believed he was stupid, and that she was smarter than he was. He couldn't get past his own interpretation of her words and used his energy to justify his anger rather than begin to watch the dishonest employee.

It is true that men are more sensitive than women about certain subjects, including their business and career. Daniel Levinson's book, *Stages of a Man's Life*, is the result of a twenty-year longitudinal study of men. His conclusion is that men need to feel successful in their career or business before they can have a successful relationship. Yes, feelings of success are deeply rooted in their career, but men are even more sensitive about their sexuality and sexual behavior.

There are indeed gender differences that cannot be ignored, and must be recognized and acknowledged. Male sensitivity in these areas is easily understood. They have very good reason to feel super sensitive. It is the man who must perform, the man who must produce, and the man who is in our society—fortunately or unfortunately—responsible for the success or failure of the sexual union.

I am not a proponent of this philosophy or belief system. I truly believe that we are each responsible for our own pleasure, and must learn how to ask for it and to get it, so that we don't blame our partner or anything else. *Sex Talk* is your guide to taking responsibility for yourself and getting what you want in the way that you want it. *Sex Talk* offers all of the techniques and behaviors that will help you to get over any impediment to your success. An example of this is the case of Cindy and Hal.

Cindy chose to speak with her husband Hal about something that had been bothering her for a long time. She felt that Hal loved her, and that she would be able to broach her request without hurting his feelings. She also felt that if she were careful, she could offer her request and succeed in her goal.

There are certain sexual issues that are discussed at the moment, in the bedroom, and during the passion. There are other issues which are less immediate, and although often more emotional, they should be discussed during an appropriate time.

Keeping these facts in mind, Cindy watched for the proper timing, when she and Hal were feeling very close and loving. She was careful to ask if he was willing to discuss an issue that was important to her. She was also careful to maintain eye contact, and she kept her hands on his knees as she spoke.

Physical contact such as this type of touch is usually an excellent connector, and ameliorates any negative feelings. Hal took Cindy's hands in his and assured her that he was willing to talk about anything she wanted to discuss. Thus the contract was established—a necessary aspect of all serious conversations.

She said, "Hal, I love you and I know that you love me. I want to ask you one favor, and please understand that this is not against you, it is for me."

Hal interrupted and said, "We've been through this before; you're just not happy with anything I do." He used the words that too many of us use when we are becoming defensive. We say "always," "never," "nothing," and "anything." Hal exaggerated the truth by stating that Cindy was not happy with anything he did. It is easy to get caught up in defending yourself by making exaggerated statements and counterattacking. She could have said, "That's not true; I love most of what you do." Or she could have become aggressive and said, "Don't put words in my mouth; that's not what I said."

Cindy could easily have fallen into the trap of defending herself and negating his remark. But she remained steadfast, determined to talk about just one subject. It was best for Cindy not to allow Hal's untrue and defensive remark to get her off track. Responding to it would have taken them both on the path of attack and defend, negativity and anger. It would not accomplish Cindy's goal. It is an absolute truth that during a conversation once you defend yourself, or attack your partner, your chances of a successful resolution to the subject are dead, gone, finished. So remember your purpose and do not fall prey to the diversions and digressions. Remain steadfast and do not get sidetracked.

Cindy followed the concept of parroting, which is to stay on track by repeating her original statement. She did not allow herself to be drawn into the argument that might have been provoked. She could have accused Hal of trying to provoke an argument, thus overstating and exaggerating his remark. It could get ugly as so many innocent conversations do. But Cindy was prepared by many of the techniques and ideas in *Sex Talk*. She did not get sucked into any diversion from her goal. She did not get defensive or argumentative. She remembered to parrot, maintaining her planned conversation. She said, "This is a suggestion that will give me pleasure and that I hope will be good for you as well so that we can both benefit from it. Can I please continue?"

Cindy was again confirming that they had a contract, an agreement to speak with each other, to listen and to be respectful to each other. Hal nodded and Cindy continued, "Hal, I love having orgasms. I love making love with you. I love all of the pleasure we have with each other, and I don't want to change anything. Our sex life is wonderful."

She reached out, holding his thighs in her hands, touching him more intimately and lovingly. "I just want to add something. I would love it even more if you would touch me afterwards. I love when you stroke my body from top to bottom. I love when you touch my breasts, and kiss my throat and hold me close. I feel almost abandoned and lonely when you don't hold me and stroke and kiss me. The orgasms are not enough, however wonderful they are—I really need all of it. I want all of it." She reached up and put her arms around him as she spoke.

Hal held Cindy in his arms and feebly apologized, saying he thought she was satisfied. He said he was tired and it was enough for him, and he said he wasn't sure he could give any more than he was giving. He said he felt devastated and scolded like a child.

It is somewhat shocking that Hal had become so defensive and upset despite the fact that Cindy had followed all of the rules of skillful sex talk. He did however, hold Cindy in his arms and stroke her hair and face as he spoke. Cindy looked up at him and touching his face she said, "What you're doing now, that's all I want." Hal heard these few words positively and constructively. Rather than hear that she wanted it to be different, he heard that he was "doing it right." His need for approval was satisfied, and her message was accepted.

Although Cindy had tried non-verbal messages, hugging him after making love, stroking him, and tucking her body into his, he had not responded. She decided to verbalize her needs and it worked. It would also have worked had she spoken of the pleasure she was feeling while hugging and stroking him, rather than not verbalizing.

The lesson is that whatever the words are, however appropriately spoken, we also need the touch, the love, the connection with each other. We need both. The lesson is that physical contact, eye contact, warm feelings, and loving messages are all part of the package of sex talk. The lesson is that how we feel about each other, how we treat each other, and how much love there is between us are all factors which directly influence any sex talk, either enhancing or diminishing it.

Of course we need words in order to express what we want both emotionally and sexually. By using both verbal and nonverbal messages we reach our partner on multiple levels, both physical and intellectual. This seems to be the best approach for achieving satisfaction and gratification, which is the goal of all sex talk.

Since we need a combination of verbal and nonverbal interactions, let's examine some of the verbal skills that are necessary for successful sex talk. I think an important aspect of our verbal communication is our interpretation, or often, misinterpretation of the words we are hearing. How often have you said something and been shocked to discover that your words were totally misunderstood? How often have you heard something that you denied or changed because you refused to accept the words?

Many men and women become involved with an alcoholic or a liar or a violent person because they refused to hear and see the clear and obvious signs of the problem. On closer examination, they remember a remark, a moment, a rumor, an actual behavior that belies their ignorance of the problem. They were not ready to see the problem since it was not commensurate with their emotional needs. This kind of blindness is not unusual or even unhealthy, although it perpetuates unhealthy relationships. It is often necessary for our own survival in that space and time.

Our defense mechanisms, such as our "selective inattention," swing into high gear to protect what we think we need at the moment. We protect ourselves from a plethora of information that does not support our emotional needs. It is also true that we hear words as "attacks" rather than suggestions if we need to feel powerful and perfect. An idea or a request can be seen as devious or controlling, and we dig our heels in, refusing to be open to it.

We are victims of our own emotional needs. Awareness of these problems can help you to avoid them. I think that some of the most critical of our verbal skills are hearing the real message, seeing the red flags, taking note of the stop signals rather than ignoring them, and addressing them verbally. There are simple rules to keep in mind so that the atmosphere in your home is one of love and connection, rather than discord and distance. Sex talk is especially powerful and effective when the heart, as well as the head, is listening.

If these rules are an intrinsic part of your relationship, your heart will always be listening.

Rule # l. Be Lovingly Honest.

See the truth and speak about it with love and respect. Do not ignore your needs—you will only build resentment and anger, and destroy the relationship.

Rule # 2. Take Responsibility for the Success of the Conversation.

Be responsible by discussing all situations. Be sure to have an agreement to speak.

- Is there enough time to complete the conversation? Is there privacy and no possibility of interference?
- Are you in a comfortable place?
- Is the subject one that will benefit both of you?
- Ask yourself these three questions: Is this for me? Is this for you? Is this for us? Be clear about your goals by taking responsibility for your purpose.

Rule # 3. Check It Out.

The following may seem humorous, even ridiculous, but when discussions are emotionally charged there is often miscommunication and confusion. It is best to check it out as follows:

- I think I know what I said.
- I think you know what I said.
- Could you please repeat what I said to be sure that you heard what I think I said?

Believe me, you'll avoid a great deal of trouble if you are sure to say what you mean and ensure that you are heard in the way that you meant to be heard.

Rule # 4. Do Not Become Defensive.

It is an absolute truth that once you begin to defend your position, there is no possibility of achieving your goal. Defensiveness closes our ears and our hearts, creating fear and discomfort. Rather than listening, we become engrossed in proving that we are *not* wrong, and that we *are* right.

Rule # 5. Do Not Attack.

Once you attack, there is no possibility of success because your partner becomes defensive. The darts and arrows you aim will miss their mark, falling on deaf ears. Unfortunately, most often we don't notice that our arrows are useless, and we continue to shoot blanks.

My father's example resonates in my brain whenever I feel like shooting one of my arrows. He said, "Remember that you have a finite number of arrows in your quick. You don't know how many, so be careful. One day when you really need one, you may reach back and find your quick is empty." It is the same concept as, "Is this the hill you want to die on?" Save your attacks; they are not only ineffective most of the time, they are destructive. See rule # 4.

Rule # 6. Be Aware of Body Language.

Watch the nonverbal signals. If his eyes are rolling or looking away, if she is crossing her arms or sitting sideways from you, if he is rifling through papers, or chewing on a pencil, there is inattention and disrespect. Your goal will not be reached without an established mutual agreement, concentration, eye contact, and respectful listening.

Rule # 7. Be Careful of Your Timing.

- Do not attempt a conversation at the "wrong" time.
- Do not share when either one of you is upset.
- Do not begin a goal-oriented conversation without considering all aspects of a successful outcome. Can you imagine asking for the delicious and romantic sexual experience you've been fantasizing about when you are both visiting his mother? Bad timing.

Rule # 8. Recognize the Power of *Yes*.

Yes is an extremely effective word. It opens doors to more contact and more experience. It allows your partner to feel recognized and appreciated. It encourages and promotes positive and loving relating. It is always a miracle to me to watch the word *yes* change a situation from disaster to success. Have you ever complained about a broken item, or a sweater that faded? If the person hearing the complaint says a simple, "Yes, I understand how upset you are," you become much calmer and more reasonable.

Sheila asked her husband to become more aware of her needs, instead of doing what he thinks she needs. Every time he said anything, regardless of his distortions or off track remarks, she smiled and said, "Yes, I'm listening." His remarks varied from, "You don't know how to show appreciation for what I do," to, "You never want to see the good things I do." After a few of these exaggerated remarks he asked her, "Tell me again what you need." She repeated her request. He asked her to be more specific, and she was.

Her, "Yes, I'm listening," encouraged and supported him rather than arguing with and refuting him. He finally was able, because of her reassurance, to actually hear her without feeling threatened.

Rule # 9. Begin Every Statement with *I*.

I need, I want, I would like, etc. If you begin with *you*, it is accusatory and provocative. For example, look at the difference in these two sentences, which are truly similar in the message, but worlds apart in affect and effect:

- "I feel very upset when you leave without kissing me goodbye."
- "You make me feel terrible when you leave without kissing me goodbye."

Take responsibility for your feelings, needs, wants, etc. *You* blames and accuses, is negative and destructive. Use *I* every time.

Rule # 10. Do Not Assume.
Remember that any assumption is a figment of your imagination. Valid or invalid, until proven to be fact the assumption is *your* creation.

- "He's looking at me as though he hates me."
- "She's really angry. I know it because she's not looking at me."

These are statements we make very often without checking to be sure of the truth. Perhaps he has a toothache. Perhaps she's preoccupied with something. Do *not* assume. It may seem strange, but it's true that most of our assumptions are not only invalid, they cause us emotional distress. We assume the negative much more often than we assume the positive. Most people think more than eighty thousand words a day. They daydream, plan, worry, etc. More than 80 percent of these thoughts are negative. Don't assume. Don't think negative thoughts.

Phil believed that oral sex was something only "bad girls" liked. This belief was so ingrained that he assumed Sally would not want him to introduce this pleasure. They were married almost seven months when Sally, embarrassed to speak about it, finally decided to do something about it. She wanted every kind of sexual pleasure, including oral sex.

She created a very romantic atmosphere, wore a sexy nightie, and told him to come to the bedroom at exactly eight PM. When Phil entered the bedroom, he found Sally lying on her back, her legs spread open and her nightie pulled up to her waist. There was a large piece of cardboard with an arrow pointing towards her vagina, which read:

"Try this delicious spot."

Phil laughed and the rest is history. He apologized for assuming what she would like or dislike.

Rule # 11. Do Not Judge.

Judgments are yet another terminator of good relationships. If you judge my behavior or my remarks, why would I want to share with you? A friend asked me why I hadn't told her that my divorce had become final. She had judged me very harshly, saying that I should be ashamed to be thinking of divorcing, and that I was a terrible person to be doing such a thing.

Why would I want to speak to her about anything, especially my divorce? We need to take responsibility for our negativity and accept the consequences. Judgments are turn-offs and often end relationships. Judgments also end any hope for open and honest sharing.

Rule # 12. Do Not Be Negative.

Negativity is a surefire way to close all possibility of successfully achieving your goal. If you complain abut a person, denigrate or embarrass them, why would they be willing to open themselves to you during an intimate conversation? Why would they be willing to give you what you want, or to even care about what you want?

Joseph told his wife that he didn't want to hear any of her requests because, regardless of what he did, she would find fault with it. Sandy admitted that she did complain most of the time and rarely complimented or recognized Joseph's attempts. He had closed himself to her because he needed to protect himself from her attacks. Being negative to another human being is actually more destructive and more demeaning to yourself than it is to your victim. Every time you make a toxic remark, you increase the amount of toxicity within yourself and push away those who love you. Negativity is a no-no—it's just too difficult to overcome.

Rule # 13. Do Not Be Sarcastic.

Sarcasm is a weak and frightened form of hurtful communication. It is only the person who is unsure of himself who needs to be sarcastic. It is caustic, cutting, and damaging, and it is used only by the inadequate and the unhappy. Don't manifest this side of yourself, even though you feel that way sometimes. We all have moments in which we want to express a mean-spirited feeling or a destructive remark. But it is best to keep those moments to ourselves, rather than lash out with sarcasm. Although some people use sarcasm in an attempt to be humorous, it almost always falls on its face. Be careful not to insult or turn off your lover with such remarks.

Rule # 14. Do Not Be Jealous.

Jealousy is extremely toxic and unproductive. If there is reason to be distrustful, that's another issue. Unfounded jealousy, possessiveness, or attempts at restraining your partner's behavior will result in anger and resentment.

We all need our own, individual, and yes, separate from each other, activities. Too often jealousy rears its ugly head when one partner wants to take a trip, or play tennis, or go fishing without the other. If you express jealousy, you express many different emotions, and none of them are love.

- You are expressing insecurity and fear of loss.
- You are expressing distrust, which is a surefire way to create insecurity and fear in your partner. If you distrust me, I begin to suspect myself, wondering why I

haven't proven my love and my commitment. If you want to keep me from something I want to do, perhaps I haven't earned your love and respect yet, and I wonder what I'm doing wrong.

• You are expressing a lack of respect. If you reject your partner's request for something he/she wants, you are not respectful of his/her needs and wants. Without respect for each other in every aspect of your relationship, you will dilute the love.

My son was very much in love with a woman whose jealousy was tearing them apart. He loved her enough to beg and plead with her to trust him and to enjoy their love for each other. She continued tantrums and hysteria each time he had to take a business trip, or plan a business dinner. Her jealousy and her inability to control the unfounded fears created a disaster. Despite his attempts to maintain his love for her, it became impossible and he felt forced to leave her.

Although it is true that jealousy does rear its ugly and destructive head very often in all relationships, if we can step back and examine it we can control it and be more loving and understanding. It is essential that you recognize that jealousy bears absolutely no resemblance to love. It is not indicative of love. It does not show love. It is merely an expression of insecurity and fear, a lack of self-esteem, and a sense of mistrust and anger. It is not in any way, shape, or form an expression of love. Too many men and women think that jealousy is a badge of honor, an absolute necessity if you are really in love. Jealousy is a badge of destructiveness and poison. It negates love, erases love, and in the end totally demolishes any love there may have been. Don't allow jealousy to invade your love. It is so toxic and so contagious that it can become impossible to control. It is basically and absolutely disastrous, with no positive aspects, and should be avoided at all costs.

During one of my lectures I discussed the tentacles of monogamy. It is often misconstrued and expanded so that we not only expect sexual monogamy, we expect monogamy at every emotional level. No one person can completely satisfy another. I may need a wonderful tennis partner or a shopping partner. He may need a friend to discuss his business with, or to jog with. It is not an act of unfaithfulness if we love the company of a person of the opposite sex other than our spouse. How boring it would be if there were no interesting and wonderful men and women in our lives other than our spouses!

Rule # 15. Do Not Compare.

Do not ever compare your lover by saying they "are just like" someone else. When you compare your lover to others, you are negating her. She is no longer unique and special and yours, she is "just like" the others. This type of statement creates a feeling of anonymity, of unimportance, and of being expendable. Words such as "just like" are to be avoided, because they erase you and your individuality, merging you with all the others. It is negative and hurtful to use this term.

Since we are extremely sensitive about enjoying the pleasures of sex talk, I feel we must establish the foundation of love and respect by following these rules as closely as possible. By feeling love, admiration, and respect we become closer and more intricately entwined with each other. These rules invoke behavior that formulates the glory and the color and the fabric of our love story. By ensuring our love story, we ensure that our sex talk will augment and intensify our story.

To offer sexual instructions, advice, ideas, or even requests is not only difficult, it is almost impossible for many of us. One reason is that we rarely know what we want ourselves. If we do know what we want and how we want it, we are embarrassed, or shy, or reluctant to ask for it. We feel that if we have to ask, it's not fair, or not worth it. We also feel very strongly that sexual requests may be insulting, even denigrating, to our lover. Our emotions tell us not to tread on sexual ground because it is sacred and fragile.

We've been taught either overtly or covertly that the sex act is too vulnerable to interrupt, instruct, or advise. It is a silent activity, an act of doing, and accepting, not evaluating. We've been taught that our sexuality is vulnerable and easily injured.

Sex talk is a problem for many couples for an infinite number of reasons, stemming from our personality, our sex education, our self-confidence, our relationship, our honesty, and our adventurous spirit. Too often we feel we don't deserve to get everything we want in the way that we want it. Probably the most prevalent impediment to sex talk is fear. We are truly afraid, and often justifiably so, to hurt feelings or ruin the moment. But the price for this fear is often very high.

Another impediment is that when we are at that moment of glory, we are not thinking at all. How can we instruct or ask or beg at that moment when we are in a state of unconsciousness, not really able to express ourselves? We need to learn the signals of our body and the signals of our partner. We need to be aware of their feelings as well as our own so that we can respond, and not need to be instructed at such exposed moments. Sex talk regarding these signals can be the answer to avoiding frustrations.

It is absolutely true that sharing our sexual needs and wants will not only enhance sexual pleasure, it will enhance the love and the overall relationship as well. When we feel comfortable enough to say the words needed to stimulate particular sexual activity, we also feel safer and more contented. On the other hand, when we hold ourselves back, we may feel frustrated and even angry, feelings that are destructive to any relationship.

Sex talk can fire your passion and your pleasure. Sex talk is yours to try, to practice, to love, and to enjoy. Sex talk is at your lips, at the tip of your tongue, ready to flow towards welcoming ears. You just have to take it out of the shadows and reap the benefits. We offer the art of sex talk for your pleasures, your successes, and your most explosive passion.

chapter 2

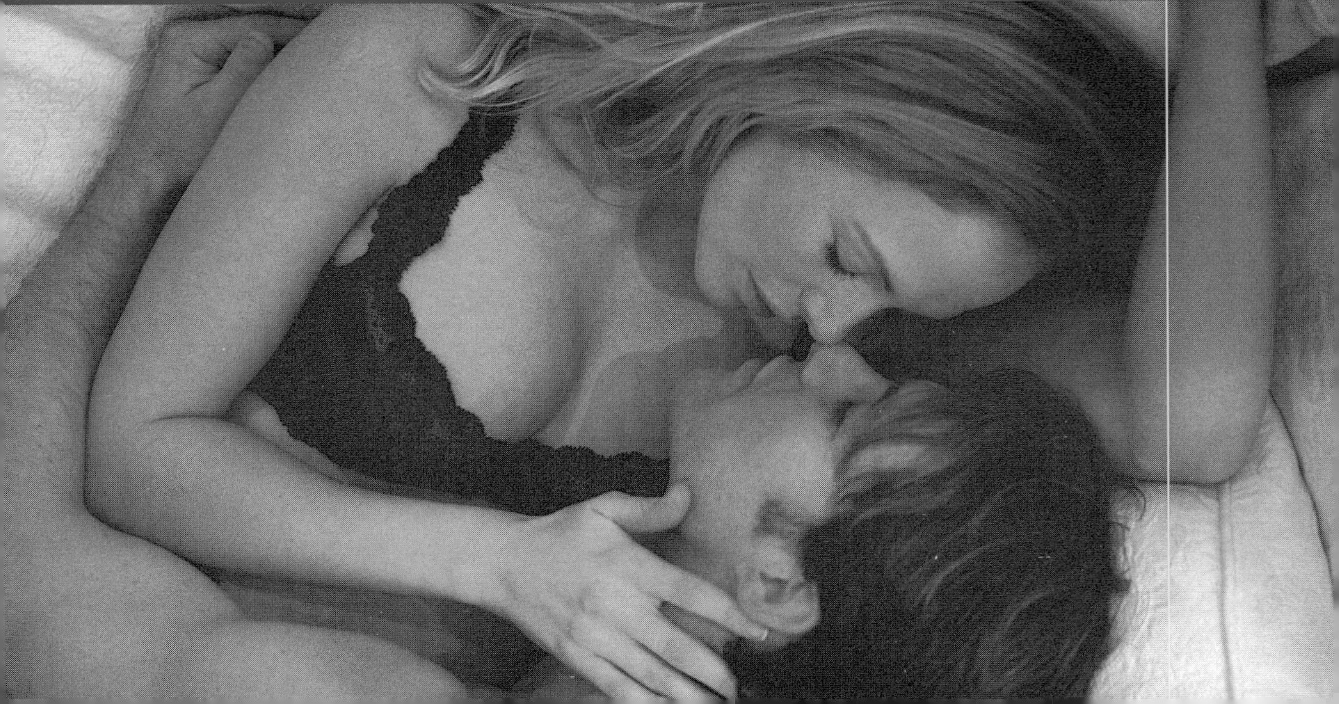

finding the words—creating the atmosphere

Because there are basic truths behind well-known adages, they have become accepted throughout the world. "Love is blind" is one of these basic truths. The blindness does not last too long, but it does create a total blackout to any behavior or situation that would bring diminishing light to what we are calling "love."

When at first we fall in love, there are no impediments, no problems, no walls too high to climb, and all imperfections, however serious, are totally and deliberately ignored.

Bells are ringing, cymbals are clanging, and screams of wild abandonment are bouncing off the walls and ceilings. I've never heard a couple complain about inattentiveness or tardiness when they are in the throes of early passion.

These behaviors are kept in the tightly closed closet of any reality that may cast shadows on the passion.

However, when the intensity of throbbing genitals and butterflies in the stomach wears off, we begin to notice those behaviors we had previously ignored. We were unwilling to notice the small things for fear our "perfect love" would disappear. After all, if we see beyond our acceptance of everything, we may not be able to continue fooling ourselves. It is especially dangerous to be "blinded" to some negatives because, when we do see them, we begin to fear the joy and the love we felt will disappear. We become so unsure of ourselves we blur reality with imagined and negative possibilities.

I've developed some ideas that may keep you from diminishing the joys of early passion. In fact, by following these ideas, you are guaranteed to maintain and enhance your love.

No Past Lovers

Do *not* ever talk about loving another partner, unless you've been married. Even after a divorce, it's best that your new love believes that this time, it's different. The thought of you loving someone else is scathing. We all yearn to feel special and do not want to be reminded of any others who may have come before us.

No Dumping

Another serious impediment to creating and enhancing passion and love is the process of "dumping." Hugo and Catherine met just after Catherine's husband died. They were very attracted to each other and began a warm and loving friendship. Catherine wasn't ready for romance and Hugo was very understanding, knowing that she needed a period of mourning before she could become more deeply involved. He was also willing to listen to Catherine as she discussed her husband and his illness. He was willing at first.

However, Catherine continued to talk about the disease, the pain, the suffering, the hardships, the agony, and every other negative she could express about her husband's illness. She detailed every doctor's visit, every medication, and every treatment. She described the hospitals and the nurses, the bad food in the cafeteria, and the long nights of waiting.

Hugo was patient, but there was a limit. One of the basics is *never* to burden another person with your problems and pain. Of course you want to share what you've been through. Of course you want empathy for your feelings, but *not* without some feeling and empathy for your listener, and always within realistic limits. You don't make it go away by constantly speaking about it. In fact, you give it more energy and perpetuate the pain for yourself and those to whom you subject the endless details. The atmosphere you create is certainly not one in which passion flourishes.

Tell It Once

Early in a relationship, explain your life, with its trials and tribulations, *once*. Do not try to assuage your own feelings by burdening someone else. It is not helpful for you to sink in the mire of your pain, and it is certainly not helpful for your relationship. If you are relentless with your confessions, do not expect another person to identify with your pain or even to empathize with you. Too many of us expect too much from our partners. We are then disappointed when they don't give us what we were unjustified in expecting. Negativity and dumping are not turn-ons. They are not happy or fun or relaxing. It only brings you both down and is truly to be avoided. If you want to share, do it with love and simplicity. Do it once and let it go.

Beware Bad Behavior

Be aware of the destructive words and behaviors that are impediments to maintaining your love and passion. Watch for the warning signs within yourself and control any behavior that will hurt your relationship. Behave in ways that will strengthen and enhance your love and avoid the others. You can do this if your motives are clear and your desire is strong enough.

It is essential that we keep in mind that nothing can happen in a vacuum. There is always the context by which each moment is surrounded. There are always the experiences upon which the relationship flows mellifluously or rocks like an earthquake. Sex talk will excite and provoke and electrify your passion as never before. However, powerful as our suggestions are, we realize that we must also create the appropriate setting. Imagine trying to make love if you're suffering all of the symptoms related to the worst flu you've ever had. Imagine trying to respond to kisses when you can't breathe, or sexy stroking when you have to rush to the bathroom. Sorry for the graphic concept, but sometimes we don't realize that our physical state does impact our passion and our sexual desire. Our emotional state impedes and even prevents passion as surely as the need to vomit. We must avoid the emotionally depleting behaviors and denigrating remarks that lower our sexual temperature and decrease our desire.

However sexy, unique, and exciting, sex talk can fall upon deaf ears if memories of mistreatment, pain, or disappointment are whirling around in your brain. It is difficult to feel inspired by the promise of ecstasy if you're stewing about an insult or a moment of neglect. Erotic promises can certainly light a fire in your loins. But however exciting your sexual promises are, if the brain is thinking of a mean-spirited remark, or criticism, or attempts at control, the necessary oxygen to keep the fire blazing will be sucked away.

Let's look at some of those behaviors that can suck the oxygen from a flourishing fire. Which rocks do we need to avoid throwing so that we establish an atmosphere of acceptance and love? Which behaviors do we need to avoid so that we don't stifle or extinguish passion and sexual energy? Remember, regardless of our motives, if the behavior is negative in any way you may deflate the power of the best sex talk.

Following are some simple but imperative reminders of behaviors to avoid, so that you maintain the high ground of love and respect. Follow these rules so that you stoke the passion and help yourself and your partner to all of the eroticism and delicious sexual delights that you know the two of you can share.

Don't Control

Respect choices without comment, whether it's which direction to take, or which food to order. Too many men and women have destroyed relationships because they dissect and denigrate. They intrude on their partner with directions and suggestions and ideas that criticize. Be proud of what your partner does and how he does it.

Paul, at 83, although delighted to find love at his age, was not willing to stay in a controlling relationship. He explained by saying, "If I want to eat ten grapes, I'm going to eat ten grapes, and I'm not going to let her tell me to eat only five."

Be nurturing and accepting, not infantilizing.

Don't Criticize

Being negative and finding faults are never productive. Often we behave poorly because we need to make ourselves feel better. Recognize what you lose when you use these tactics, and cherish what you gain by avoiding these and other hurtful behaviors.

Cheryl couldn't understand why a man she dated just once never called her again. She spoke of all the things they had in common; their laughter, their three-hour dinner, their delicious kiss at her door. Upon further questioning she said she'd recommended what he should eat, which glass to drink his wine from, and even suggested that he wear a lighter sweater because restaurants are often overheated. As she spoke a light bulb went on. She realized how critical she'd been and that it would have been a miracle if he had called her again.

Don't Brag

Don't be a braggart, ignoring or neglecting your partner to build your own ego. If your partner is constantly talking about achievements, looks, wonderful jobs, high incomes, new cars and apartments, it is difficult to feel that he values you and what you are offering to the relationship. It is also often embarrassing to be with such a person. There are very few narcissists who have enough energy to have successful relationships—they are too intent on relating to themselves.

Don't Judge

No one enjoys being told they are wrong, foolish, inexperienced, or negative in any way. Keep the peace with your loved ones by listening and watching without judgments. Don't expect your partner to be open with you, to share feelings and needs, if you are judgmental. Too many people dismiss a heartfelt fear or need by saying, "Oh, you don't mean that," or, "That's no big deal, you can get over it." Be careful how you respond if you want to share emotionally.

Don't Be Stingy

Don't be stingy with your time, your compliments, your attention, your empathy, and your cooperation. Being generous takes very little effort and reaps boundless benefits. In fact, recent research indicates that the absolute most essential characteristic of a happy person is generosity. This conclusion makes sense because when we are satisfied with ourselves, when we feel full and complete, we have a great deal to share. Be generous. Be happy.

Don't Withdraw

Refusal to discuss an issue or to deal with a request for a discussion is a slap in the face. It is painful and rude and takes a heavy toll on our ability to respond lovingly. Don't be aggressive, demanding resolution or explanation. Be loving when discussing a serious topic, be kind and attentive. Listen and respond, rather than attack and defend.

By establishing this kind of loving and respectful atmosphere of communication between you, your sexual lives will fly to the stratosphere because of the positive energy you are continually exhibiting. Imagine creating a continuous sensation of pleasure and joy with smiles and compliments and strokes and loving remarks. Sex talk is your key to creating these continuous sensations. Sex talk is the magic carpet on which you can fly to the apex of sexual pleasure.

We use sex talk to excite, to stimulate, to tease, and to promise. It is incredibly exciting, creating moments of passion which are more inflamed when sex talk is part of our lovemaking. Words are turn-ons that fire the body, turn on the juices, and stimulate libido.

Silent sexual connections are not as thrilling, nor are they as explosive. This is true because words and sounds stimulate our minds. It is true because our intelligence makes us responsive to language. Sex talk is an essential aspect of our lovemaking. It does what it promises, and it adds to the excitement of each and every moment. Sex talk stimulates during sexual pleasuring. It also fires the body with promises of the future. Anticipation creates a great deal of heat.

Sex talk, when used appropriately, gets us:
- What we want
- When we want it
- How we want it

So what is the canvas on which we draw the perfect setting in which sex talk will be as powerful and delightfully satisfying as it should be? It is within your power to avoid the negatives that nullify the benefits of sex talk. It is also within your power to utilize the behaviors and thought processes which enhance your love, your devotion, and your passion. I feel it is simple because I have developed the three R's for a perfectly loving and supportive relationship. They are:

Respect

If you act at all times with respect toward your lover, you will avoid any negative, cruel, and mean spirited behaviors. Respect precludes name-calling, neglect, broken promises, or discourtesy. If you behave with your lover as you behave with your boss, colleagues, friends, and clients, you will behave with respect. Would you ever call your boss "stupid"? Would you ever walk by a client without saying hello? Would you ever criticize a colleague because something was broken or forgotten? I don't think so, because you show them respect. It is also true that when you respect yourself, you behave respectfully to all others in your life. Don't manifest disrespect for yourself by behaving that way to others, especially your lover. Act with the regard and consideration you expect for yourself, and then luxuriate in the atmosphere of pleasure you've created.

Shirley and Leo are one of the happiest couples I know. They promised forty-seven years ago that they would always say "thank you" and "please" to each other. They do, and it has worked wonders for them, and it will for you as well. This symbol of respect overflows to other aspects of this admirable behavior. I've never heard an unkind word or seen an unkind gesture between them. Their two sons are equally happy in their own marriages. We emulate our parents, behaving as they do and as they expect us to. You give your children a wonderful legacy and style of life when you are respectful to each other.

Reward & Recognition

Be generous with compliments. Recognize a meal well prepared or a new hairdo. Be proud and attentive to a new job, a good tennis swing, or a happy smile. Be aware of his new suit or tie, shave, or weight loss. Be aware and recognize the behaviors with attention and compliments. We take each other for granted too often and for too long. Don't be a taker without giving back. Compliments and attention, recognition, and appreciation are simple, easy to do, and extremely beneficial for both you and your partner. Think of a compliment as a magic carpet on which you both soar with happy feelings and smiles. Think of a moment in which you show appreciation as exquisite music that sounds out the love you feel. Realize that a simple compliment tells your partner that you are aware and appreciative and in love.

Response-Ability

I think of responsibility as the *Ability to Respond*, and spell it accordingly. If you are able to respond to your lovers needs and wants, are responsive to feelings and behaviors; see the body language and the fear and the love and the pain and respond to it, then you are showing your love. You are showing your integrity, your devotion, and your desire to be all that you can be for the person you love. In return you will be in flow with each other, connected with the powerful desire to be there for each other, to care for each other, and to substantiate all that you feel for each other.

Love Contract

Make the following contract with yourself and your partner:

- I will make our relationship as positive and nourishing as it can possibly be.
- I will behave with love, consideration, and caring.
- I promise to solve any problems with respect and consideration, not anger and attack.
- I will make all of our sexual experiences as glorious and uplifting and connecting as I possibly can.
- With this contract I promise you my love and my devotion to making all of this a reality for both of us.

Now You're Ready

Let's go on to how to use sex talk with the knowledge and the determination that all of our words will be positive and loving so that all sex talk will inspire responsive passion. We want our sexual pleasures to be hot and juicy, completely satisfying and ecstatic. Sex talk will make this happen.

chapter 3

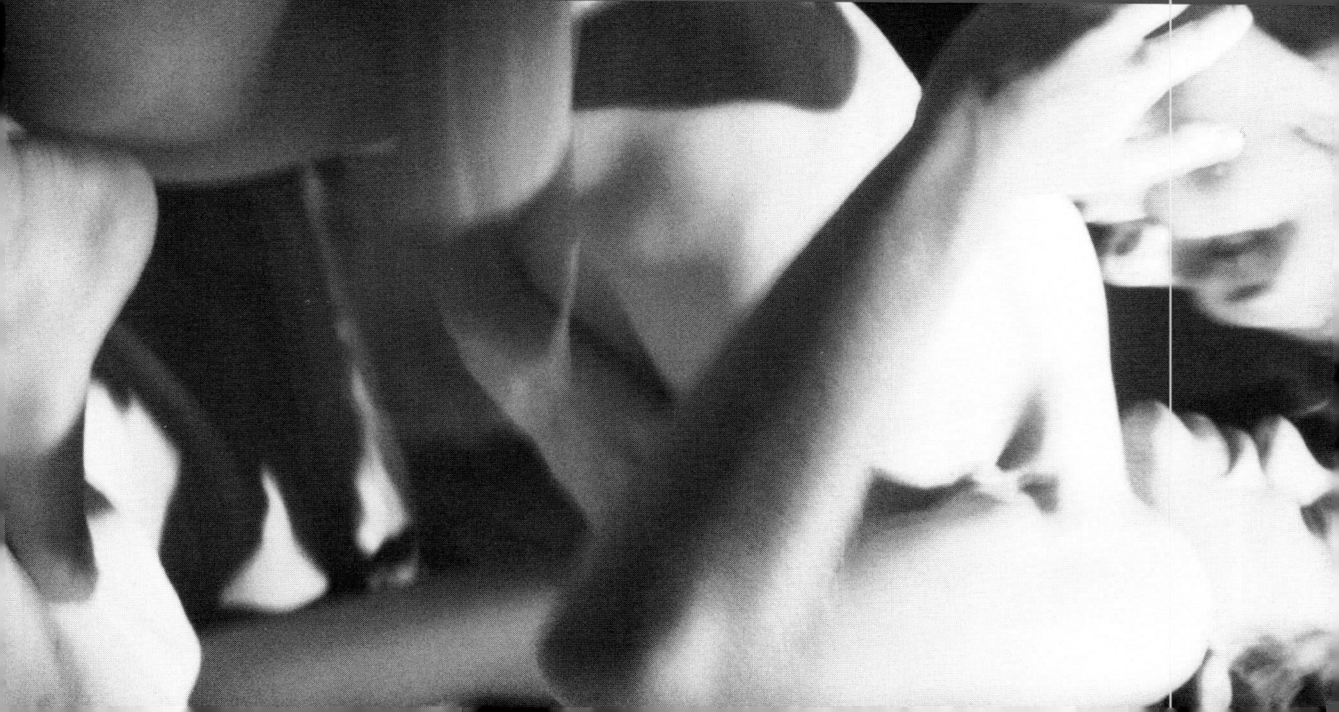

what you
want and how
to ask for it

It became obvious, as I peeked into the sexual lives of those men and women that I questioned, that sweaty skin, thrusting bodies, sucking or plunging, touching and kissing are, of course, essential components of good sex. What my research for *Sex Talk* uncovered is that there is an additional aspect of continuing good sex. The responses indicate that when you include your sexual dreams—what you've always wanted, wished for, and fantasized about—you add a dimension of passion and satisfaction that is not only incredibly valuable, but seems to be an absolute necessity for sustaining sexual pleasure in many relationships.

The sexual act and our feelings of sexuality involve a multiplicity of behaviors and desires. We are incredibly diverse and complicated, with various levels of passion, degrees of tension, and mysteries created about our sexuality. Therefore, when questions are asked about our sexual behaviors, the responses are diverse and complicated as well.

Because of our limited understanding of our sexuality, because of our attitudes and belief systems, we've constructed pathways of safe areas. Too often these safe pathways are so limited that our sexual behaviors become boring and ordinary. The culprits are numerous: our background, our religion, our culture, and even our own inadequacies or low self-esteem.

We have a medley of judgments, criticisms, fears, and inhibitions that have caused us to build barriers to certain behaviors. Because of our reticence to set ourselves free from the bondage of judgments and inhibitions, we restrict ourselves from certain potentially satisfying and passionate sexual behaviors, although they may be the answer to our boredom.

Sex Talk is a roadmap, a guide to discussing your sexuality in every aspect. It is a guide to sharing not only your needs and wants, but to sharing how, when, and where you want your needs satisfied. Sex talk can motivate you to consider opening yourself to more of the wealth of innovative, original, and appetizing carnal sensations available to you.

Responses to the question, "What do you want and how do you get it?" have indicated to me that there are two categories of sexual pleasure. The first category is the sexual experience that most of us have, most of the time. We kiss and hug, we penetrate and suck, we touch and love, and of course we enjoy every moment.

The second category is similar, with the added pleasure of imagination and newness, adventure and exploration; it is a journey into the unknown, the dream, the fantasy. The intensity of the experience is enhanced because it is your fantasy, your dream, your hope. It is fraught with anticipation and illusion. It is a fulfillment of what had previously been merely a mirage.

Because of our need to enhance and perpetuate our passion, we must realize one basic truth. All of the sexual experiences that pleasure our bodies pale in comparison to the ecstasy we can reach if we pleasure our bodies *and* our minds more completely and elaborately by using our fantasies and imagination. Those men and women who responded to my question by detailing how their fantasies were fulfilled, or how they explored a new sexual territory, or how they used creativity and artistry, planning scenarios, etc., seemed to be much more sexually satisfied and much more sexually oriented. Their partners responded in kind because they felt loved and cared for.

Each time a man sets the scene for love and romance, the female responds more positively than if he says, "C'mere honey." Each time a woman allows her passion to take over, lets her inhibitions to fade, and plans for an incredibly wild and sexy experience, the male responds with a hard and ready erection, as well as with more love and excitement. It seems an absolute truth that the use of creativity and imagination can and will open the doors to your sexual freedom, your sexual expression, and of course magnified sexual ecstasy.

Ordinary and Extraordinary Sexuality

Included in the first category are kissing, penetration, oral sex, touching, various positions, and so on. This type of sex seems to be more simple, more prevalent, and easier to speak about.

The second category, that of creative, imaginative, adventurous sexuality, includes all of the above with the added twist of adventure and art—a blend of the mind and the body in styles and behaviors that are unique to the adventurer, special to the artist, created by the dreamer.

These sexual experiences seem to require more time and thought, but are almost always more extraordinarily passionate and extensive. These sexual experiences are less common in that there are fewer men and women who use their minds and imaginations to create a fantasy, and there are fewer men and women who are valiant enough to try. Even those who are creative revert to the everyday sexual experience the majority of the time. They explain that using fantasy, planning elaborate and adventurous sexual experiences, is time consuming and not practical in everyday life.

The payoff is that these experiences, however infrequent, succeed in fending off the boredom that too frequently erodes sexual experience and the achievement of the highest level of sexual fulfillment. The concentration and determination required to experience unusual and exhilarating sex seem well worth it when the results are described. Those who go the extra mile seem to add a great deal of fun to their experiences and feel that they remain more connected emotionally and romantically to their mates.

If you look through the keyhole of a couple in love, a couple who is touching sensitively and warmly, moving in and out of each other's bodies and kissing with delicious mouths and loving feelings, you will enjoy the scene. Such routine lovemaking between a couple can lack depth and ingenuity, newness and creativity, and though it may satisfy basic impulses, it can become dull. A ho-hum sex life—without mixing some wildness into the more usual and comfortable sex—can hamper a couple's intimacy. Do not think for one moment that one type of sex precludes another. Comfortable, usual, ordinary, and frequent sex is as essential to a good sex life as the wilder, more passionate, explosive kind of sex. Sexual pleasure should never be denied however you get it, whenever you get it, and as often as you can get it. Waiting for screaming, writhing, sweating four-hour orgies is a mistake. Don't say no to any sexual pleasure, regardless of any limitations that may be present.

If you think of the scenes of sex which really excite you, make your blood pressure rise, your heart beat faster, and your juices begin to flow, chances are those scenes involve people who are wild with passion, attached to each other with flailing arms and legs, open mouths and keening sounds. It is not only in the movies or books that this type of sex is experienced; it is within the realm of real life as well. Wonderful as it may be, sex talk does not suggest waiting for such moments.

Those who are lucky enough to experience this level of sexual explosion are deeply rooted in the gestalt, the connection of body and mind. They are linking the fabulous sensations of the flesh to their deepest, most personal and intimate emotional needs. It is in this realm of mind/body connection that sex flourishes and is continuously exciting and delicious, because the mind adds a new dimension to the experience each time.

What They Want and How They Get It

When I asked men and women, "What do you want and how do you get it?" many responses were in the realm of everyday sexuality, and described the majority of our sexual experiences.

"I take his hand and put it where I want it."

"I touch him the way I want him to touch me and where I want him to touch me."

"I just tell him. Let's face it, if we love each other, we can talk, can't we?"

"I try to be gentle. I know it's hard to talk about certain things."

"I like questionnaires; they are impersonal and non-threatening, so I use them to get my point across."

"I like to read magazines together, *Penthouse* and stuff like that. I tell her I like this idea or that idea. We began putting food on each other's body parts after reading about that in a magazine. It is fun to do, and very sexy."

"I kiss him on his mouth the way I want him to kiss my vagina."

"I move my body so my position is good for me, raising my legs or even putting a pillow under my behind."

"I tell him, harder, or more, or that's good. He loves me to talk and moan; if I seem to be giving instructions, he doesn't mind, so I just say it."

"I probably push her sometimes, putting her head down to my penis or pulling her legs up. Now that I think about it, maybe I'm a bit rough, but we have a lot of sex so I guess she likes it."

"I'm not sure what I like until she's doing it, then I just tell her that it's great. I wait for the great things and then say it. Incidentally, I say that pretty often."

"We've been together for nine years. Now I can give him a look across the room and he knows what I want, and we leave the party or restaurant and he proves that he knows what I want."

"I like to write him notes, describing what I want him to do, or what I want to do to him. Yesterday I wrote that I wanted to taste the skin behind his knees. He told me that his legs wobbled when he read it."

"We have signals, scratching his shoulder is harder, and tapping my finger on his shoulder is softer. If I want more, I just say it, and if I like it I pretty much scream—I'm a screamer."

Beyond Every Day Sex

Following are some of the responses to the same question that involve planning, fantasy, imagination, and creativity. These responses indicate how the power of your mind can provoke a level of sexual exhilaration far above and beyond what is felt if the fantasy is not included.

"We have a contract to try something new every single week. We take turns creating the new scenario. I get my ideas from books, TV, etc. She seems to conjure up incredibly sexy experiences. One night she made herself the 'treasure' and I had to follow her clues in order to find her. Each clue described something she would do to me if I did find her. Of course I did."

Her clues (Note: They walk through their bedroom closet to their bathroom):

1. You can't eat here, you'll make a mess—but you carry what I love to eat with you.
2. The clothes are here but you won't need any. Licking is for nude body parts.
3. Now go right through, the water is running—soap and lotion await you.
4. Then it will be your turn to do what you will with me.

This describes a fun experience. Imagine the anticipation and the wonder as you follow the clues, imagine the explosion when you find the treasure.

Angie writes, "I think that sex should be as spontaneous as possible to be really exciting. When I want something I plan it, but make it seem like it just seemed to happen. I always wanted to make love in public, but I didn't tell Robbie about it. We were going to a wedding in an outdoor park. I realized it would be dark, everyone would be intent on the wedding ceremony, so it was a perfect time. I wore a long coat and matching dress, with no underwear. I took seats on the far right, well out of the lights from the altar that had been set up.

"Everyone was concentrating on the ceremony, I quietly moved onto Robbie's lap, my dress and coat flowing around me, cloaking our secret. I leaned back and began to unzip Robbie's pants. He didn't take long to get the idea, and his cock slipped out of his tuxedo pants and directly into my wet and waiting spot. I sat quietly as he pumped into me until we both climaxed. I was more excited about fulfilling the fantasy than the actual stimulation. I realized that great sex is not always what is happening, but where it is happening, and what it means to me.

"Robbie was so excited he burst his bubble within two minutes. He couldn't believe the excitement of 'doing it' in public. He said the best part was that it was a total surprise to him. For me the best part was that we did it. He also admitted that if I'd discussed it with him he would have thought it was stupid."

Angie's fantasy is far from unusual. The fact that she planned what she wanted and made it seem spontaneous also is not unusual. Many men and women are not comfortable speaking about certain sexual desires, so they develop a system by which they get what they want, without too much talk about it. Others truly feel that talking about it will dilute, even diminish the experience. For others who are free to say what they want, the discussion and the shared planning makes it even more exciting, adding to the experience.

Paul loved satin and was much more turned on, more passionate, and more satisfied sexually if satin was part of his lovemaking. He had always bought his wife satin nighties and underwear, but one day he realized what would add to his sexual pleasure. It was so simple, he laughed at himself. He bought several sets of satin sheets in various colors. He described the sensation of slipping and sliding into ecstasy, absorbing the delicious touch on his skin, smoothly floating through the most passionate and rewarding sex of his life.

Sometimes, it's as easy as a purchase. What material will do this for you? What scent? What color? What sound? Make it happen. Buy it and use it; allow it, whatever it is, to augment and intensify your sexual pleasures. Free your mind and your thoughts, allow them to soar, to explode, to become your reality. Your sexual reality will roar with the addition of dreamed moments and fantasized sensations.

Another reply highlighted how simple it is to introduce a new technique or behavior without jeopardizing your relationship, or hurting his or her feelings.

Hillary always wanted to add the concept of bondage to her sex life, but was afraid it might go too far, or that Ted would think she was crazy. One night she played Sharon Stone. She wrapped Ted's wrists lightly with a large silk scarf. She positioned the scarf so that it covered his eyes as well. He was surprised and began to speak but she covered his mouth with hers and immediately mounted him.

She said, "I was so hot I couldn't stop loving him, licking and sucking, moving from on top of him to eating his cock, to mounting him again. He responded with equal passion, turned on by mine. My only regret is that I waited so long to use what had always been a fantasy of mine. Covering his eyes was a last-second idea, and he loved it because he said that it added an element of fear and unknown to the moment. I'm so glad I opened myself and fought my fears and insecurities. Ted loves that I'm a 'hot tomato,' as he calls me. He doesn't think, as I thought he would, that I'm a slut or crazy—not at all."

Jami had always wanted to experience a threesome but he was afraid to mention it to his wife. He finally broached the subject by describing a "friend" of his who had sex with his wife while a girlfriend watched (just watched). Jami's wife, Alana, didn't buy it for a minute. She described it as "sick" and thought the wife of the "friend" should get divorced immediately. Jami didn't get upset or argumentative. He merely said that it is only a fantasy, something to dream about, to add an element of excitement to their sexual moments.

Jami was amazed that night when Alana began stroking her pillow and moaning words like, "Oh your tits are so beautiful. I love how soft your skin is. OOOOHH your cunt is so wet," as she moved her finger in and out of the pillow as though probing a vagina. Jami was so excited he described entering Alana and exploding in a climax more powerful than he'd ever had. Alana had realized that they didn't have to bring the fantasy to any reality since the fantasy is powerful enough to add that extra special dimension to the experience. She loved Jami enough to want to satisfy his fantasy, without giving up her own needs and values.

Rhoda told me that her fantasy is to have sex with another woman, but she would never actually do it. However, when she and Bernie are thrusting and thrashing, she purses her lips and begins sucking into the air as if she is sucking on a vagina. She actually puts her tongue out and licks and sucks. These motions add to her pleasure to such a degree that her release is, as she described, "exponentially better than if I don't pretend to be sucking on 'her'...whoever she is."

She added that sometimes she sucks on the space between Bernie's thumb and finger, since it is indented and simulates a vaginal opening. This too seems even more exciting than if she sucks into the air. Bernie does not know the thoughts and images that are provoked by Rhoda's sucking motions. She thinks, however, that he is more stimulated because he imagines that she is thinking about sucking on him.

Vivian and Wally were friends for many years. They had never felt a sexual attraction to each other but always enjoyed being together. One day Vivian told Wally that she always imagined having sex with a man she would call "Daddy." He pulled her to him and kissed her with a hunger she couldn't believe. He told her that he always wanted to have sex with a woman and call her "Mommy." They began a wildly inflamed relationship.

Why had Vivian withheld this fantasy for so many years? Why was Wally so inflamed by it? It doesn't really matter, and the truth is that there is probably no one answer. The situation points to very valuable information. Too often we do not admit to ourselves or to anyone else the sexual fantasies that would add so much to our pleasure and perhaps add to our partners as well. Share your fantasy, share what you want in the way that you want it. Take the risk. Your dream may be fulfilled, as Vivian's was.

Wally and Vivian have lived their fantasy again and again, each time with more excitement and satisfaction. Their fantasy has been fulfilled and their bodies respond magically and continuously to the words they use. Some of their favorites are:

"I love fucking you Mommy."

"Suck my tits Daddy."

"Put it in now, now Daddy, now."

How sad it would have been if Vivian hadn't shared her fantasy, and they had never found the passion and love they now feel for each other. She told me, "I have no idea why I said it, and what would have happened if I didn't say it. I'm only happy that I did."

What is it that you are holding deep within the inferno of your loins? What is crying to be released and satiated? Do it.

Say it. Plan it. There truly is a pot of gold at the end of the rainbow of fantasy and sexual exploration. Some fantasies seem strange, unusual, even weird to others. Yet to those who integrate their fantasy into their sexual life, the pleasure is extraordinary.

Burt is incredibly turned on if he is wearing makeup. Maryann benefits from his passion and has accepted his choice. They both enjoy the fruits of satisfying Burt's pleasure at wearing makeup since it adds so much to their mutual satisfaction. Maryann had been ready to divorce Burt, fearing that he was homosexual or weird. However, she came to realize that her love for him was stronger than her distaste for his preference. She was able to accept his desire to wear makeup and it was extremely beneficial for her since he was so much more sexual, so much more often.

Pat loves whipped cream and he loves his wife. He has found a way to combine the two so that they both enjoy an orgasmic and delicious frenzy. His fantasy of eating whipped cream from a belly, or a breast, or an ass, is satisfied again and again. Tina is more and more pleasured, more and more joyful that Pat includes his fantasy in their lovemaking because it improves and adds so much to her pleasure.

Stan approached Cynthia with the following scenario: "I know you'll think this is strange, but I would love to put an egg into your vagina and watch it come out of you." Cynthia was appalled and rejected the idea immediately. However, Stan asked again and again, and finally Cynthia said, "All right, just once."

They were making love when Stan suddenly and without any discussion placed an egg into Cynthia's vagina. She laughed, saying that it was cold and that it surprised her at first. Stan stood up and asked her to push as though she was in labor.

As Cynthia contracted her vaginal muscles and expelled the egg, Stan actually had a climax watching her. His long-term fantasy had finally been experienced and his thrill was beyond description. His love for Cynthia was expressed again and again, verbally, nonverbally, and in every sexual pleasure he could imagine to show how grateful and happy he was.

Cynthia actually enjoyed the feel of the egg inside her and the feel of power she experienced as she expelled the egg. Her vaginal muscles were tested and proven strong and effective. Her love for Stan was proven as she satisfied this strange request. Her sense of power was also enhanced since she felt personally responsible for Stan's sudden and explosive climax without any stimulation other than the visual picture of the egg leaving her body. Her sexual pleasure was multiplied exponentially since Stan's passion and love for Cynthia was expressed wildly and passionately.

Is this a strange fantasy? Perhaps it is to most of us. But to Cynthia and Stan it is an addition to their sexual scenario that multiplies and expands their love for each other and their physical pleasure with each other. The moral of their story is that however strange you may think your fantasy is—share it. You never can tell how wonderful it may be for both of you.

What do you want and how do you ask for it? Are you afraid to share your innermost sexual thoughts and images? Do you use your mind, your imagination, or your creativity? It is an absolute truth that your most powerful sex organ is your brain. Use it.

Do you avoid asking because you don't even know that special something that will send electric currents throughout your body? Do you avoid asking because you haven't decided what "else" you want to add to your sexual experience? Do you not even think about it? Do you avoid asking for fear of hurting his or her feelings?

Think now. What is missing from your lovemaking?

- What would improve it?
- What would add to your level of passion?
- What would add to your loving, to your completion, to your satiation?
- What do you want?
- Is there something else that you need?

Try this exercise to discover your deepest thoughts, your physiological responses, your most sensitive spots, your emotional needs.

- Lie nude and touch your body.
- Allow your mind to flow with the movements of your fingers and hands.
- Allow your thoughts to fly away from reality, away from the moment, away from what you already know.
- Touch yourself everywhere, in places you've never touched. Touch yourself in ways that you've never touched. Touch yourself with fabrics you've never used. Find a piece of velvet, of satin, of cotton. Find a feather, a soft brush, a hard brush. Touch yourself to stimulate your body and in turn stimulate your mind.
- Use your mind to focus as you explore every part of your body. Which fabrics excite and please you? What type of touch do you like here, and what type of touch do you like there?
- Insert your fingers into your mouth, your ears, your vagina, your anus. What pressure do you prefer? How far do you like to penetrate? Feel the difference in the tissue, the musculature, the softness, the hardness.
- Feel your teeth with your tongue, experience the smoothness compared to the corrugated roof of your mouth. Taste your tongue, your lips, your gums.

- Make small circles on your body with soft fingers. Make larger circles using more pressure. Make long straight lines with your fingers along our arms, your inner thighs, your throat and face. Use varied pressure, use a variety of touch.
- What have you never done before? Can you do it now? What have you never felt before? Can you feel it now? Suck on your finger as you wish she would suck on your penis. Suck on the indentation between your thumb and finger as you wish he would suck on your clitoris. Become aware of what you like, love, need.

Know your own body, your own preferences, your own dreams. Explore all that you can about yourself so that you can phrase the right questions. Be aware so that you can ask for the prize you *know* you want to win. Help your partner to find the golden treasure you've been hiding from yourself.

You can't reach what you want until you know what it is that you want. Many men and women remarked that they like kissing. Others said they love to be touched. Others said they love oral sex, or hard penetration. Of course, we all love and want these behaviors, but are we getting them in the way that we most want them?

Is oral sex as it should be for you? How do you want to change it? One woman responded, "I suck on his lips the way I want him to suck on my vagina." This is yet another way to make oral sex much more satisfying for you.

Tap on his shoulder if you want it harder or softer, as one woman does. Do you know when you want it harder? Do you know how you are most satisfied?

As you touch yourself and allow your imagination to flow fluidly, deeply into the realm of fantasy and pleasure, seek to break down the wall of inhibition and fear. Look into the depths until you see a pool of passion that is yours for the drinking, yours for the touching, yours for the asking, and most importantly, yours for the taking.

Seek the new, the unusual, the difficult to discover, the imagined thrill that will most entice and arouse you. You can only do this by discovering for yourself where that dream lies, where that pleasure center is.

How would you answer the question, "What do you want and how do you get it?"

Plan some exciting responses. Think through the scenario of explosive and exquisite connections with the person you love, with the body you love. What would that be? How would you feel? Can you have it? Do you deserve it?

Sex Talk is a book about you, a book about who you are, what you want, and how you can get it. All of the information, all of the research, all of the descriptions point you in the direction of self-discovery, an inauguration of passion and lust, a key to the sexual being within you. It is up to you to follow the path towards what is sexually best for you. Remember, this is not a dress rehearsal. This is your life and it is up to you to live it to the fullest with the most ecstatic and fervent joy you can possibly generate.

Get what you want. Get it the way you want it. Get it right and get it often.

It is all fantasy, all imagination, all adding to the experience of the mind, to the experience of the body. Every aspect of your personality, all that is within your capacity to love, to think, to feel, is yours to enhance and to embellish.

Use every skill you have, all the energy you have, and all of your determination to have a more pleasurable life. You will find that as you reach deep into the recesses of your mind and emotions, all that you feel and have will be improved.

• Your pleasures will intensify.
• You will understand and fulfill your needs.
• Your life will flow.

This process is not only successful, it is explosive.

Use the exercise above. Use the scenes you've peeked into as you read this chapter. Use your mind. Let go of your fears and inhibitions. Be sexually alive, vibrant, and fulfilled.

chapter 4

sexual needs– pleasures and vulnerabilities

Our sex drive is not an isolated commodity that is separate and apart from our feelings, our moods, or our attitudes. Sex desire can suddenly flow from your heart to your loins with a touch of a finger, a glance, an aroma, a smile. Desire is fragile and vulnerable; it is not a given and it is not impermeable to everything in our environment. In fact, it is very dependent on everything in our environment. Our sex drive is dependent on our moods, our attitudes, our feelings, and our physiological state. In fact, our sex drive is delicate, even frail.

Recognizing that this is true, sex talk encourages and details all of the ramifications of sexual energy, sexual pleasure, and essential sexual desire. We feel it is our responsibility to create the mood, setting, and atmosphere so that all sex talk will be lovingly received and accepted. We suggest that you remain respectful and loving, rewarding and caring in every room of the house if you expect the fires to be roaring in the bedroom. We suggest that you be totally and absolutely aware of each other's feelings, moods, and needs, so that sexual pleasure is always on the menu and sex drive is always part of the recipe.

We do this by reminding ourselves of how much we love each other, and how lucky we are to have each other. Remember your contract to make your relationship as positive and nourishing as you possibly can.

It is always a good idea to cancel any negative thoughts with positive ones. If you are angry or upset about something, if your job is too stressful or there are money problems, think about the good things at work and the financial security you do have. Not everything is wrong; think about the positive sides rather than the negative ones. If your relationship is troubling you and your partner is upset, sit down together and remember your wedding day. Talk about how you looked, what you wore, the guests at your wedding, how you proposed, why you proposed, and how you felt when you said "I do." You will begin to smile at the memories and the negative will feel less important because you can face them together just as you did on your wedding day.

Remember the day you first met. Remember your very first kiss, your very first sexual connection. Remember all of the love, kindness, and exuberance you felt and still feel for each other. Don't allow one moment or one situation to cloud all of the good that is between you. Rather than exaggerate the negative, perpetuate and embroider the positive. Share your feelings about the first time you saw each other. Share how excited and thrilled you were as you waited for that phone call, that first date, that first vacation together. There is so much in a relationship that can conjure the good and the positive if you will remember to do so rather than wallowing in the muck and the mire of everyday disappointments and problems. Thinking positive is being 95 percent ahead of any problem; try to use this absolute truth as often as you can.

The success of your sex talk is directly dependent on your continual acts of love and affection, respect and kindness. With these factors in mind, based on the atmosphere of love and acceptance you have for each other, you can now begin to share your innermost sexual needs and desires. You can share these within the walls of intimacy and safety which you feel for each other, without fear of judgment or rejection. You can share your most secret desires and needs. You can be open, honest, and without apprehension because you are emotionally secure with your love.

This chapter is about the nitty-gritty of what you want and how you want it. As I've said, sex talk is very effective and is a sure-fire way to stimulate sexuality and sensuality. Sex talk, when used in the right setting at the right time, will absolutely bring you and your partner all of the pleasure and satisfaction you both want.

Sex talk begins with an understanding of each other, an agreement to share in an anxiety-free atmosphere with feelings of safety and comfort. When this atmosphere is established, all of your sex talk will be much more effective. Establishing this setting is an essential aspect of all relationships.

By sharing basic information with each other, you create these feelings of safety, openness, and understanding. I suggest the following experience to help you to build a safety net between you so that your sex talk will be accepted and enjoyed. This safety net will also strengthen your willingness to share and to be as provocative and sensual and tantalizing as you can possibly be. By sharing this information, you will break down inhibitions and fears of rejection.

Let's face it, we wouldn't bake a soufflé or cook chicken soup without a recipe. Yet we continue to make love with each other without knowledge and awareness of the intricacies and innermost needs of ourselves or of each other.

Create the recipe. Have all of the ingredients at your finger-tips. Have all of the proper tools and equipment. Have it all, know it all, and use it all. The results will win awards from the greatest sex experts in the world, the two of you!

This very explicit and open sharing is best done in a neutral atmosphere, with loving words and mutual goals. We can accept suggestions more easily in neutral, non-threatening surroundings. By sharing the following details, you will avoid the need to correct or change or improve a specific sexual act at an inopportune moment. By sharing these preferences and needs, you will know the right spots, touch the way your partner wants to be touched, and be aware of the what and the how at each sexual moment.

It is probably most effective if you complete these questions separately. Sharing the information and discussing various issues will be exciting and provocative, frightening and embarrassing. But it will be effective since both of you have recognized the need to learn about each other. You have also accepted the responsibility to respond with respect to each and every request.

Too often, there are unspoken desires, unexplained needs, and even special behaviors that we would like to share, but feel reluctant to do so. These questions will help you to open up to each other in a non-threatening and failure-safe atmosphere.

Now it is time to actually respond to the following questions. After you have written as many responses in as much detail as you want to, exchange papers with each other. Since it is best to keep this exercise as neutral as possible, it is suggested that you avoid the bedroom, which is fraught with expectations, memories, and intimacies which may interfere with your communications. The living room is too frivolous, with TV, lounging couches, and soft pillows. This hopefully will be a profound sharing of desires and pleasures, not done with a careless attitude. The bathroom is too uncomfortable and usually too sterile. The kitchen seems to be the most neutral, the most comfortable, and the most likely to induce you to accomplish the "work." Many couples prefer to share in an outdoor or public setting so that they continue the work without interruption.

What is the work? The work is the sharing of your deepest sexual needs and the most intimate experiences that give you pleasure. Too many couples continue to touch in ways their partner doesn't enjoy; kiss with too much tongue or too little moisture, thrust too quickly, or fellatiate too loosely. There are positions we know we prefer, movements we enjoy, and others we don't. These are difficult issues, not only because the subjects are fragile and the topic often embarrassing, but also because there is always the fear of hurting each other's feelings. In addition, we have not really explored some of these sexual issues for ourselves. Often we don't realize our own sexual potential or preferences. We rarely delve deeply into these issues for ourselves or for our partners.

Do you really know what touch you like and where you like it? Is a circular lick good in one spot, but not in another? Is a kneading with the knuckles exciting in one place, but hurtful in another? Are fingers more fun when they are wet or when they are dry? Is a tongue a wondrous body part or can it be annoying or even unpleasant?

Have you ever examined your body closely, looking, touching, licking, or kissing various spots? Think back to your responses to the exercise in Chapter 3. Do you really know the sensitive areas, the turn-on spots, and the turn-off spots? How can you share what you want and how you want it until you discover these things for yourself? Be absolutely honest and as aware as possible when you consider this questionnaire. The more you know about yourself and your pleasures, the more you will be able to share with each other, and the more you will be able to be passionate, exciting, and satisfying to each other.

There are so many sexual issues to learn about your partner and about yourself. Often these are too difficult to discuss. First, agree to respond to these questions, and sit quietly together as you do. Begin the exploration, the hunt that leads to the treasure chest of sexual delights.

You may want to respond to these questions verbally, sharing with each other spontaneously and immediately as you read the question together. You may want to be more specific and write the answers on a separate piece of paper. You may even want to get very serious and use your computer to detail your responses.

I believe the last suggestion will be most helpful and productive because you can be as complete and as intense as you want to if not restricted by verbal communication or handwritten responses. However, I suggest that you discuss the task and decide how you both want to continue.

Intimacy Contract

Please realize that we cannot read each other's minds. Therefore, I suggest another contract.

- You may not like what I like—I accept that.
- You may not want what I want—I accept that.
- You may not want what I want *when* I want it—I accept that.
- You may want to tell me what you want—I accept that.
- I may want to tell you what I want—Is that all right?
- When I ask for something I am not telling you what to do.
- When I suggest something I am not criticizing you.
- When I need something it is not because you do not satisfy me.

- When I want to change something, it is not because I don't like it, it's because I like it more in a different way.
- I want to tell you everything because I want you to tell me everything, so that we can satisfy each other.

Introduction to the Sex Questionnaire
The entire purpose of this questionnaire is for you to be able to accept directions, ideas, and requests so that you can give and get what you want, when you want it, and how you want it. What's the sense of giving something that's not being enjoyed with all of the relish with which we're giving it? What's the sense of not being aware of perfection in what, how, and when? There is beauty and exquisite pleasure in perfection, and by knowing each other completely and sensitively, you can create perfection.

Questionnaire Contract
- We agree to complete these questionnaires as honestly and completely as we possibly can.
- We agree that if there is a question we *do not* want to discuss, we will skip it. We will respect this request without judgment or negativity. (Many women and some men do not consider anal sex a negotiable topic. They refuse to discuss it. Often these feelings change, but must be skipped if either party is not comfortable

discussing any question. It becomes off limits by request and the request is non-negotiable.)

- We agree that we will respect each request and attempt to satisfy each request. If there is something we don't feel we can satisfy, we will discuss it without reprimand.

- We agree to list any behavior, however unusual or seemingly impossible, so that we can learn more about our needs and wants.

- We will share the completed questionnaire and discuss our responses, calmly, lovingly, respectfully, and without judgments or anger.

Pleasure Evaluation

Following are some behaviors to trigger your thoughts so you can be really specific, share exactly what you like, and perhaps learn about yourself as you respond. It is true that we don't really concentrate on the sensations and pleasures of the flesh. Perhaps by being specific about body parts and variety of stimulation possible, you may become more specific in your responses to the questionnaire. Write your preferences and share your responses after each section.

1. Kissing.

Here is what I like when we kiss:

a. Upper Lip

b. Bottom Lip

c. Corners of my mouth

d. Tongue

e. Face

f. Ears, Nose, Eyes, Cheeks, Chin

g. Throat, Neck

A sample response:

a. I like you to put my upper lip between your two lips.

b. I like you to do the same with my bottom lip.

c. I like you to lick the corners of my mouth, and to run your tongue across my lips.

d. I like you to explore my mouth with your tongue, along my teeth, my tongue, the roof of my mouth, all over.

e. I like you to suck my entire mouth into yours. I don't like you to kiss my face for too long, I like mouth to mouth most of the time.

f. I get crazy when you lick my ears, especially if you go inside. Leave my nose out of it, I don't like that. I do like it if you run your tongue along my eyelashes, that's fun. My cheeks and chin don't matter.

g. My throat is a very sexy spot and I like you to lick it, but after we've kissed. I love you to kiss my neck while we're cuddling after sex.

2. Touching.

This is what I like when you touch me:

a. Soft, gentle touch

b. Deeper, more massage-like touch

c. Circles, small or large

d. Hair-stroking

e. Part of my body I would prefer you not touch

f. Massaging with oils and lotions.

g. What other touching do you want? How and where do you want it? If you don't ask, you may not get it!

Sample responses:

a. I like soft, gentle touches most of the time. I like long stroking motions. For example: from shoulder to wrist, from breast to thigh, etc.

b. I like hard massaging before we begin to make love, as though you are taking care of my body, rewarding my skin. I like you to use your knuckles, hard and tight into my muscles.

c. I like you to make little circles on my eyebrows and along my cheeks.

g. I love it when you explore my body as though your

hands are measuring tapes or flashlights or an X-ray machine. Pretend I'm a dark cave and you have to find all of my crevices and treasures. Ignore my "sex" zones and explore every part of me. Find spots you never knew existed.

An infant is polymorphous perverse, which means that every inch of his body is excitable and pleasurable. He learns very soon that there are "special" areas such as his genitals, because he is diapered. Unfortunately he also learns that it is a "special" area because his mother rubs and strokes and kisses every part of his body *except* that part. We develop what we call erogenous zones.

However, it is still true that we can be and are polymorphous perverse. If we stimulate all parts of the body, we can become excited and pleasured. So please, don't just dive for the "specials." Roam around, do some reconnaissance, make a total map of *every* area, touch and kiss, and lick, and fondle, every single inch of each other.

Ivan loved the back of his knees licked. Julie never knew that before responding to this questionnaire. Ivan himself had not thought to share it, he thought it so silly.

Inside the elbows, between the toes, in the armpits, the sole of the foot, inside the knee, the ear lobe, the back of the neck, along the spine, etc., etc., etc. What are your "hot spots" that are not usually considered erogenous zones?

3. Penile-Vaginal Penetration.
   This is what I like:
   a. My favorite position is_____
   b. I also like_____
   c. Play with my testicles during/Play with my clitoris during_____
   d. If I want you to hold my balls tighter I will/If I want you to go harder I will_____

The idea is for you and your lover to recognize your sexual needs and share them. The more you talk to each other about what you like and yearn for, the more the conversation may whet your appetite to be open, graphic, and decisive. Do you remember a moment when you were in a fit of ecstasy, all pistons on high alert, all systems go, and you wished for just one small difference—one touch here, one lick there, or one hard squeeze which would have made the moment even more exquisite? Do you remember wishing he would move just a bit, or rub harder, or kiss this or that? Do you remember hoping that she'd hold tighter, or suck longer, or move more? By giving each other all of the information requested below, you will avoid these moments of frustration.

Think of these moments and share your needs, so that next time he will remember to lick your nipple and she will remember to grab the base of your penis, just the way you like it. Explaining specifically what you like in this non-threatening atmosphere will help you to avoid those more sensitive moments when you don't feel comfortable asking for whatever it is.

The Sex Questionnaire

1. When we make love I need you to_____

_____

_____

_____

You may need kissing, hugging, or stroking during foreplay. Please be as specific as you can so that your partner understands exactly what you need from him/her.

Phyllis wants to be kissed very gently on the lips and face. She feels very cared for when Steve does this.

Joan cannot be turned on until she hears Sam speak words of love. She can feel her fluids flowing when he says, "I love you."

Chu needs to have her nipples licked with long hard strokes, not soft circular ones, before she is "ready."

Karen feels unloved until Rick gets an erection and tells her that he never was as hard and as ready as he is with her. She loves him to say, "You did this baby, it's all yours," while he rubs his erect penis against her belly.

What do you need? What is your absolute necessity? What turns you on that you cannot do without?

2. **When you do what I need as described in question 1, what do you want me to do?**

_____

_____

_____

Phyllis wants Steve to kiss her face and lips gently. While Steve is doing this, he wants her to hold his penis and stroke his testicles. They both share their desires, therefore satisfaction is mutual.

While Lon is licking Chu's nipples the way that she loves it, he asked that she play with his ears and hair. Lon loves when Chu strokes his hair and ears. It makes him, as he says, "very hot."

3 . I want you to touch_____

It is interesting that many men and women love to be touched in certain areas, but not in others. We don't always tell our partners which are which. Detail the parts of your body that you want to be touched. Detail *how* you want to be touched there.

4 . I don't want you to touch_____

There are body parts that are ticklish, or embarrassing, or too sensitive, or just uncomfortable when touched. What are they? Be specific, be honest, be sensitive to your own needs.

5 . During intercourse I would like_____

_____

When you are in the throes of passion, thrusting and heaving with each other, a touch, a move, even a word may interfere. What interferes with your pleasure during intercourse? What enhances your pleasure during intercourse? Do you want your balls played with? Do you want your nipples licked? Do you want your body stroked and touched? Do you want soft touches or hard touches? You may prefer silence, sex talk, dirty talk, or descriptive talk. Think about what you truly enjoy and what enhances your pleasures during thrusting.

Stan loved sex talk and used it very often, but during thrusting he would be absolutely silent. Mary couldn't understand why his words of love and passion were suddenly silenced. Stan explained that he needed to concentrate so that he could maintain his erection and please her for longer periods of time. Any interruption was an interference to his pleasure and to the enjoyment he wanted to give Mary. When he explained this, she was not only understanding, she was relieved. She'd thought his silence meant that he wasn't enjoying himself.

$6.$ **Do you like to masturbate before, during, or after sex?**_____

_____

Do you enjoy masturbation while with your partner? Do you want to watch him/her masturbate? Do you enjoy mutual masturbation, pleasuring yourself while he pleasures himself, or pleasuring each other at the same time? Many men like to ejaculate at least once before penetration so that they can thrust for longer periods of time. Unfortunately, most men will masturbate without their partners' knowledge. Sharing this desire will help you both enjoy the masturbation with sex toys or without them.

It is also true that women are multi-orgasmic. Any climax will enhance the ability to continue to climax. Since it is difficult to orgasm during penetration, an orgasm during moreplay with the help of a sex toy will enhance her ability to climax during thrusting. Masturbation in any form will also encourage orgasms during oral sex.

$7.$ **Do you want to use sex toys?**_____

Explain what you would like to do with these and when you would like to use them. What are your favorite kinds of sex toys? Do you want to play with a vibrator, a dildo, a strap-on, or just a feather? What else, if anything, do you want to do while you play? Do you want to be cuddled and stroked? Be as specific as you can and also as imaginative as you can.

8 . How do you feel about kissing body parts?

_____

_____

_____

Describe which parts you like kissed. Which parts do you like licked? Which parts do you want ignored? Do you like hard kissing on one part and licking on another? Do you like a body part to be sucked in completely or merely "tipped"? Be clear about the different types of kissing on different body parts.

9 . Do you mind if I let you know what I need you to do at that moment of no return?

_____

_____

_____

Janet loved when Greg went down on her, but too often she would lie there wishing for a bit harder or a bit deeper. She and Greg made up signals so that she could nonverbally let him know what she wanted at the moment. He knew that she had specific needs and he was willing to satisfy them without feeling like a failure or that he was "doing it wrong."

Greg was able to share that he also needed specific motions and pressure when she sucked on his penis. By signaling to each other without judgment or negativity, they both enjoyed their own specific pleasures with freedom and without any of the previous frustrations.

10. What is your favorite way to signal that you want to make love?_____

_____

Many couples have signals which are obvious only to them. If at a party, or when with the kids or company, you may want to signal each other privately that you are suddenly turned on and want to go home. What is your favorite signal when you are alone? Do you want to begin kissing or hugging? Do you want to begin by lighting a candle? Do you want to run a hot tub and invite your lover to join you? What beginnings turn you on? What is your fantasy beginning? What do you wish he/she would do to let you know sex is on his/her mind?

Remember that it is a fallacy to expect that our sexual experiences are always spontaneous and need not be planned. We cannot read each other's minds and very often we need to tell our partner what we want, when we want it. We need to entice and seduce. We need to provoke the feelings in each other. How do you want to entice? How do you want to be enticed?

11. What are you absolutely opposed to? Is there any sex act that is out of bounds for you?

- Many women are opposed to making love with the lights on.
- Many women are uncomfortable giving head or having men come in their mouths.
- Many men and women are opposed to anal sex.
- Many men and women do not participate in sado-masochism.
- Many do not like domination types of sexuality.

If one of you would like something that the other does not, you may want to consider trying it out. If not, you must both agree to ignore and forget the request. There is a very effective sexual therapy technique known as desensitization. If you are not totally against something and want to explore the possibility, you can learn how to become more open to sexual experiences you may not have tried before. However, as I've said, if it's a *no*, then leave it at that.

12. Do you enjoy role playing during sexual acts?

_____

Who do you want to play? Who do you want your partner to play? Many men and women spice up their sexuality and sensuality with role-playing. If you are given a contract to play Marilyn Monroe tonight, imagine how much more sensual and exciting you can be. Role-playing helps you to lose inhibitions by putting on a mask and opening yourself to the adventure.

13. Are you interested in a threesome or group sex?

_____

This is one question which is usually a non-negotiable and skipped by most couples. However, there are couples who would like to try this but have never had the nerve to verbalize it to each other. This question gives the opportunity to do so if the thoughts have been there.

14. Are you interested in videotaping or photographing your sexual acts?_____

_____

Many men and women enjoy watching turn-on films. Imagine watching a film of yourselves. Would that be of interest to you? According to *Men's Health Magazine,* 56 percent of men surveyed reported videotaping their sexual acts. Is this one of your pleasures?

15. What turns you on visually?_____

_____

Are you interested in watching porno films, browsing X-rated Internet sites, or looking at pictures? Be specific. What types of films do you especially want to watch? If you're not sure, what would you like to try? Would you like to go to an adult video store and browse the offerings? Do you like to look at pictures in books or magazines? What poses and types of models turn you on the most?

16. Do you like sex talk during sex? Do you like romantic talk? Do you like dirty talk?_____

_____

_____

Give examples of words and phrases you like. Do you want to have these whispered in your ears? Do you like to moan or scream and do you feel you have the freedom to say whatever you want or make any noise you want?

17. Do you like "show time"?_____

_____

Would you enjoy watching me dance, sing, or be seductive? Do you like specific clothing, costumes, nighties, police uniforms? What show would you like to see? Do you like exhibitionism? Do you want to watch your partner doing sexy things? What do you want him or her to do—masturbate, play with a sex toy, eat a juicy peach?

18. What is your favorite sexual setting?_____
_____

Wild passion in the tub or shower? What about the kitchen table if he "just can't wait"? Do you like dangerous encounters? Would it excite you to have sex in a hospital bed in the room next to the friend you're visiting? Would you enjoy lying on the satin cushions in the church prayer room? Do you imagine making love on a plane or bus? Do you prefer the privacy and beauty of your bedroom with aromatic candles and flower petals on the sheets? Where is your favorite place?

19. What else would *you* like to tell *me*?_____
_____
_____
_____

20. What else would you like *me* to tell *you*?_____
_____
_____
_____

When you've completed these questions, shared and discussed the responses, please do the following:

Put your arms around each other.

Look into each other's eyes.

Kiss a long and delicious kiss just the way you like it.

Complete this one last sentence:

I feel that our lovemaking is_____

_____

_____

_____

Use delicious and passionate and positive words to describe it.

chapter 5

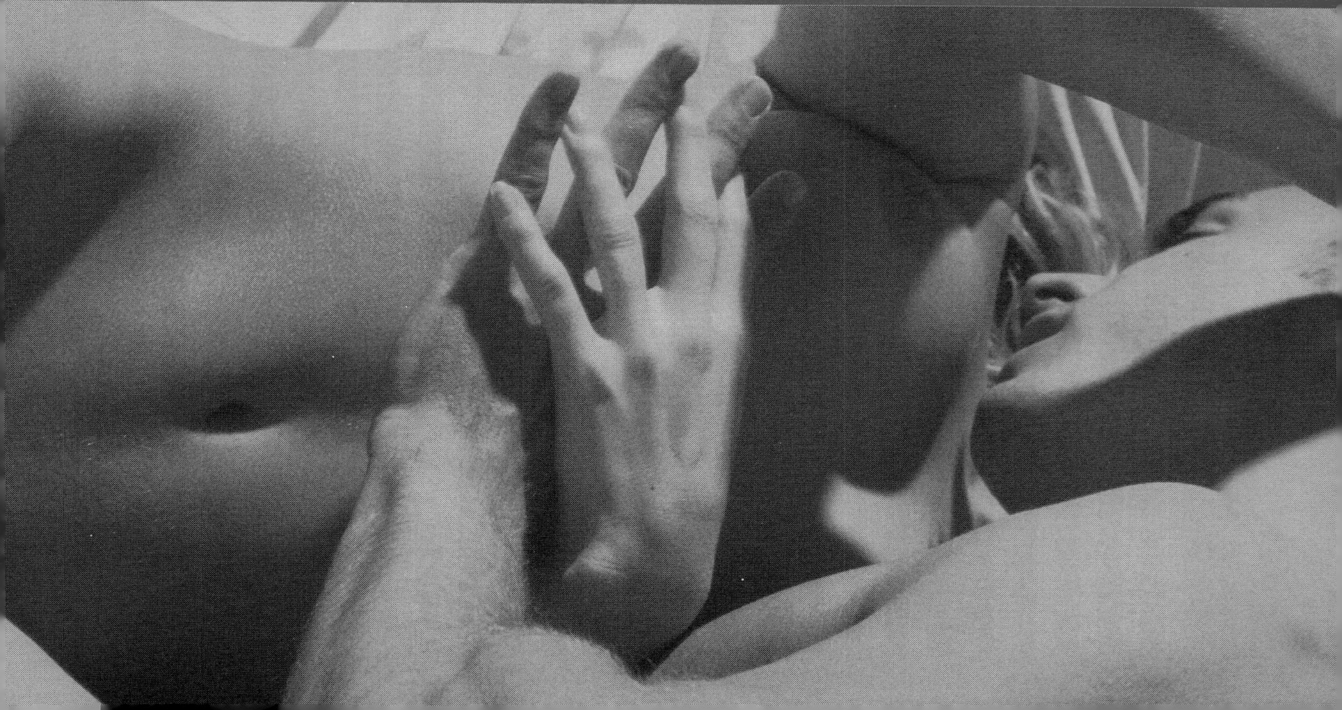

sexual pleasures—body part by body part

We are first and foremost human beings with heart, mind, and soul. We are flesh and blood, *and* feelings, *and* wants and needs, *and* hopes and dreams. We are a complex totality of emotions, thoughts, and body parts. Our humanity encompasses all this.

We are also compartmentalized physically, a conglomeration of separate body parts that need various stimulation and various attention. Our body parts are differently sensitive, and have particular needs at different times and in different situations. We have what are known as erogenous zones—areas that are particularly sensitive. These areas actually change when stimulated—they feel and look different. It is the erectile tissue in these areas that creates these changes. These areas seem to demand and receive the most attention during sexual experiences. We almost always kiss mouths, lick nipples, suck genitals, penetrate the vagina, rub the penis, and so on. In fact, it is interesting that when I ask a couple how they make love, they invariably tell me step by step what they do and how they do it. It seems to become ritualistic, written and directed prior to the moment, followed as though a script. Too often, this kind of rote behavior becomes boring and our interest in repeating the "performance" wanes.

By including all of your body parts, and paying attention to all their various possibilities, we can change the script and create more passion, excitement and interest.

Perhaps we pay special attention to certain areas because we can actually see the evidence of our successful lovemaking. Our genitals become engorged with blood, developing a darker skin tone and a swollen appearance. The erectile tissue changes the texture of the skin so that the nipples become hard and seem to be wrinkled. We can feel the juices flowing within the vagina and see the penis harden and lengthen. Other physiological changes occur, which are not as easily visible.

For example, there is even erectile tissue inside the nose which, when stimulated, causes the nose to "run." As proof of how powerful your sensations are, you will notice that when you are eating an enjoyable meal your nose will suddenly begin to run. It is evidence of the stimulation of the erectile tissue due to the pleasure your taste buds are experiencing.

In fact, when you are born, your entire body is what is known as polymorphous perverse. Every inch of your skin is so sensitive and so aware of the stimulation available to it, that any touch, any movement, any sensation at all can be intensely and exquisitely pleasurable.

Infants love being touched and do not differentiate the pleasure of the touch because of where it is. They enjoy the holding of the fingers, the stroking of the belly, the kiss upon the brow. In fact, infants have orgasms, small spasms of pleasure when touched. You may notice an infant rocking himself against the mattress of his crib, or rubbing her legs back and forth against each other. You may also notice a tiny shiver, a motion of small shaking, which is actually a climax. We know that infants *in utero* have orgasms, and we know that infants enjoy all types of stimulation. What further proof do you need to believe that our sexual lives are natural, necessary, and an integral a part of our physiological and emotional needs?

There are many alternatives, many styles, and many approaches to sexual pleasure. Life is a smorgasbord of pleasures—pick and choose, but do not neglect. Remember that sexual pleasure is a built-in health care system and is necessary for complete health. In his book *The Function of the Orgasm*, Wilhelm Reich describes the moment of climax as the *only* moment in our lives during which we are completely relaxed and feeling a sense of internal peace. When we climax, our blood pressure improves, our heart muscle strengthens, the acidity in our stomach diminishes, our muscles become relaxed, and our sense of well being is enhanced. The orgasm is not only a pleasure, it is a necessity for our health.

Many men and women who have spinal cord injuries lose their ability to be sexually pleasured or to climax. Recognizing how crucial this pleasure and physiological release is, the medical community has integrated physical therapy with sexual therapy. These men and women can actually re-learn to experience sexual pleasure by concentrating on an area not affected by the paralysis. I worked with a young man who had become paraplegic as the result of a motorcycle accident. Despite almost total paralysis, he actually learned to experience a climax by concentrating on the back of his neck. While he concentrated, using a fantasy, film, or magazine, his partner would touch the back of his neck, pleasuring the exact spot. With the combination of the fantasizing, the concentration, and the stimulation, he experienced a sensation very similar to an orgasm. There was no ejaculation or erection, but the body reacted in much the same fashion with a spasm of release and a sensation of intense pleasure, and the same positive and healing physiological release.

Body parts are each as deliciously sensitive as you would like them to be. There is no need to concentrate on the so-called erogenous zones when it is true that we can enjoy the pleasure of the flesh on every inch of our bodies. In fact, the skin is the largest erogenous organ we have, so why ignore most of it to focus on just a few areas? It is also true that when we stimulate any area of the body, the erogenous zones react. Juices will flow, the penis will harden, and the nipples will contract if you are licking a knee or sucking on a finger. Each area of our body, however isolated during stimulation, contains nerve endings which travel to all areas of the body, therefore creating the excitement and passion that is so delicious.

Let's look at some of the areas of the body that are too often neglected. How and what can we do to stimulate and pleasure all of each other and all of ourselves? You've already examined what you like in Chapters 3 and 4. You've thought about how you like to be kissed, how and where you want to be touched, and what you really enjoy. Perhaps you've overlooked some areas that may give you even more and actually elevate your level of lovemaking to a higher and more electrifying degree of pleasure.

The Neck

The most sensitive area of the back of the neck is directly in the center, from the hairline to the top of the spine. Run your tongue along this soft and somewhat indented area. Watch his hair curl and her body begin to purr. Use a feather to stimulate just under the ear, around the base of the neck to the other ear. Use your tongue or a finger, tasting and touching the soft skin. Watch the response of your partner. The area is so sensitive, and so virginal to attention, that your efforts will be extraordinarily rewarded.

The Feet

I know some of us don't enjoy having our feet touched, licked, or rubbed. But if you do, it can be an extraordinary source of pleasure. Try gently rubbing your knuckles along the sole of the foot and just under the toes. Rub your fingers between each toe, gently pulling and relaxing the usually unattended toes. Take the ball of the foot in your hand and circulate it, moving it around to stimulate the entire foot, bringing the blood flow to the feet, warming them and loving them. If it pleases you and your partner, take one toe at a time into your mouth, lick the toe and suck on it. You may use this action to teach your partner how you like to be sucked and licked in other parts of your body. Use sex talk to tell him that you'd love him to do as you are doing when he is going down on you. Use sex talk to tell her that you'd like your penis attended to just as you are attending to her toes. Demonstration is like a picture—worth a thousand words.

The Chest

It is common to pay attention to the nipples, circling your tongue around the delicious spot, feeling it harden and wrinkle under your tongue. Try doing the same just along the outer rim of the chest, in the tender spot where the arm extends from the chest. Touch just under the arm along the outside edge of the chest—lick, use fabric, feather, mouth, and fingers. Touch along the throat, paying attention to the Adam's apple area, the slight indentation along the bottom of the throat. Knead the top of the chest where the shoulders meet and feel the muscles relax under your hands. The chest has many parts and too often we neglect what may be our most pleasurable spot. Pay attention to all of it. As one woman told me, "I like to leave no hair unexamined, no spot unseen, no piece of him unlicked."

The Hands

The hands are of special interest because you can make love to them wherever you are and whatever situation you're in. However public the situation, you can always manage to hold his or her hand and send messages that are wildly suggestive and incredibly exciting.

The center of the palm is very sensitive and can be stimulated wherever you are. In fact, rubbing your finger gently across his palm can stimulate his thoughts to what you will do once you leave the party, meeting, or dinner. A touch of promise along the inside of the fingers can work wonders on the imagination and have her juices flowing even before you reach home. Remember, sex talk can be non-verbal as well as verbal. Use as many gestures as you can to say how excited you are, how passionate you feel, and how much you want her. Send your messages through the fingers in the most delightful, yet private, way possible. Take each finger between yours and rub up and down as though it were a penis. When you are in a private and intimate situation, use your tongue in the same way. Again, as with the toes, you can demonstrate how you like to be licked and sucked.

The Stomach

There is a thin line of hair from the belly button to the genitals that I like to think is there to direct us to the pleasure spot at its base. A tongue from the belly button down, slowly, with little flicks, and small breaths blowing on the spots to be licked, will create a level of passion and sexual need which will drive him or her into a frenzy. Don't go for the "spot" too quickly. Tease and taunt with your tongue as you run your fingers along the edge of his waistline, along the line of her hipbone, along the outline of her rounded belly. The best of sex occurs when there is a push-pull feeling of giving and taking. Lick and suck, blow cool air, and touch gently, bringing his temperature to a boil, creating a rhythm in her hips and buttocks, and raising your own level of desire to immeasurable heights.

The Knees

The backs of the knees, though often neglected, are incredibly sensitive and therefore can enjoy stimulation to the fullest. Use your knuckles to rub the inside of his or her knees. Tenderly rub back and forth inside the pocket just behind the knees. Take your finger and gently make a line from his knee down the back of the calf to his ankle. Move your fingers around her ankles, paying special attention to the area around the outside bone. At the bottom of this bone is a sensitive small patch of skin that loves to be licked and stroked. Take both hands and encase her legs from the ankles to the knees, using your fingers as though on a piano keyboard flicking up and down. Return to the soft skin just behind the knees and give it your all, with fingers, mouth, tongue, and teeth. Love the spot and your partner will love what you're doing to it.

The Thigh

It is surprising to me that many of the couples I speak with do *not* pay attention to the responsive and tender spot just inside the thigh, from the pubic hairline to the side of the knee. Gently run your finger along the inside of the thigh and you'll get those bells and whistles, the writhing and the purring. It's a great spot and too often ignored.

The Buttocks

Cup the behind in both your hands, just underneath, holding it like a precious package. Run just one finger along the bottom line from the outside of the buttock to where it joins the genital area. Tease back and forth, coming closer and closer to the vaginal lips or the testicles and penis. Run your hands just along the buttocks, tantalizing your partner as you approach the pubic area. Do this slowly so that you know how much your partner wants. Watch the reaction as you pull and push, give and take, stimulating that soft and needy spot, reaching towards it. If you're so inclined, do the same with your partner on his or her stomach. Run your fingers along the buttocks, coming closer and closer to the anus. Stimulate the edges of the anus, making circles around the darkened skin, the erectile tissue surrounding the anal opening. If you'd like, run your tongue along the circle of skin, driving your partner into a frenzy of passion and perhaps even to climax. This area is so sensitive and so emotionally charged that it is not uncommon to experience a climax during the rimming of the anus with your tongue. Again, tease, give and take, lick and blow small waves of air, lick again. The buttocks and the anus are also too often neglected by many. Remember, it is just skin, and all skin needs and loves attention.

The longer you experience the loving and touching, the sexual moments before penetration, the more your muscles tense, the more engorged your genitals become, and the more fulfilling and powerful your orgasm will be. So tease, go slow, wait and tease again. Enjoy the delicious flavors and the passionate needs you stimulate as you explore every inch of the entire body, from head to foot, leaving no inch of skin untasted or unfelt.

chapter 6

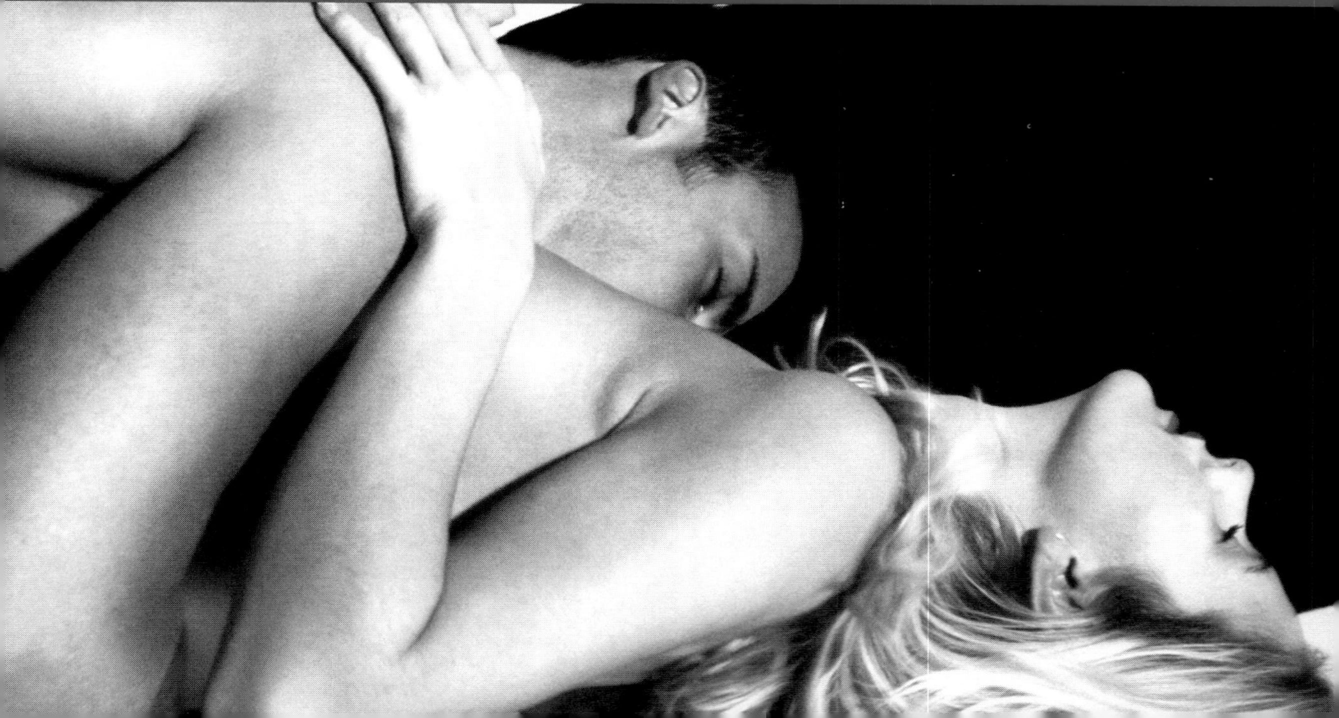

the sounds
of sex

The hottest show in Las Vegas is *Zumanity*. It is an imaginative show by Cirque du Soleil which flaunts fabulous beauty, physical talent, and every form of sexuality you can imagine. There is sadomasochism, homosexuality, lesbianism, and autoeroticism. There is apparent nudity and seduction, sexuality in its rawest form. In general, *Zumanity* is a show for the voyeur, the passionate patron of the human body, and the fun-seeking tourists in Sin City, Las Vegas.

Most interesting to me was the reaction of the men and women I questioned after they saw *Zumanity*. The one scene that was preferred by more than 90 percent of those I questioned was the scene with the "sounds."

The scene was accompanied by the most seductive, tantalizing, and titillating sounds. There were not only moans and groans, but high pitched squeals, deep panting, and guttural sounds of release. There are no words, but the sounds are perfectly translatable and understood.

A very beautiful, seemingly nude woman is hanging from leather straps, high above the audience. She is literally tying herself in various positions with these leather straps. She wraps them around her ankles and hangs from her feet. She gyrates into position to wrap her wrists and hangs from her hands. She actually hangs from her neck, held only by the straps she has placed beneath her head. In the end, her body is totally shrouded by the straps, flat on her back, her legs and arms dangling. The scene ends as she lies totally sheathed in the leather straps, high above the audience.

The sounds of sex, the guttural sounds of struggle, the high pitched squeals of fear, and even the keening of pain define her emotions, and tell the story as clearly as though there was a narrator. These graphic sounds hold the audience in a state of passion and tension. Finally, the deep moaning, sighing, and heavy breathing of exquisite delight are as much a release to the audience as is her own orgasmic quaking and trembling.

When the scene ends the audience is in a state of paralyzed silence for several seconds. Finally they burst into thunderous applause accompanied by shouts and whistling. It is as though the entire audience is experiencing its own orgasmic release.

It would have been simple to describe the magnificent acrobatic feat of this very beautiful, apparently nude woman. But when asked to describe their favorite scene, their remarks did not include her looks, her movements, her gyrations, or her acrobatic skills. They described their favorite scene with remarks directly related to the "sounds of sex." It was the vocalization, the aural stimulation, the expressions that seemed to rise from her belly and her soul that the audience found so evocative.

People's responses were like this:

"Oh, what a fabulous show—that scene with the woman making those sounds, that was the best."

"Those sounds really drove me crazy. This sure was the best sex show I ever saw."

"Why even ask, while that woman in leather spun around above us, there wasn't a single movement in the audience. We were spellbound by those sounds, what great sounds she made."

The sounds of sex are what this book is all about. The sounds of sex are recognized as the gunpowder in the bullet, the lightning to the rod, the natural Viagra to the body. What sounds do we love? What words do we want to hear?

What is the turn-on? We know how important, even essential, it is to make sex talk an intricate part of the passionate experience. Let's start with some practice. However silly or unnecessary it may seem to you, ask yourself these questions and take part in these exercises.

Sex Sounds Questions

1. What sounds do you make during sex?_____
   _____

2. What sounds would you like to make?_____
   _____

3. What sounds would you like your partner to make?_____
   _____

4. What music do you like to hear when making love?_____
   _____

Sex Sounds Exercises

You may find these exercises may turn you on. Sounds can do that. Our physiology is very responsive to aural stimulation. Although the female is more responsive to words and sounds than the male, both are stimulated and pleasured by words and sounds. Watch your own body as you take part in these exercises. Please don't be a voyeur to these words. Take action. Make the sounds mentioned. Hear your own interpretation of the moan, the groan, or the scream.

Do you like how you sound? Do you emote with these sounds as you make love? Do you want to add any of these sounds to your passion? Listen to the sound and watch how your body responds. I know you will be amazed to feel your physiological responses as you vocalize the various tones, pitches, and inflections. Some sounds may seem silly and make you laugh. Other sounds will actually stimulate your libido, and others will make you feel very seductive. As Nike says, "Just do it." Watch the results.

Moan

Listen to how it sounds. Does it sound the way you want it to sound? Practice. Moan a bit throatier. Moan a bit longer. Moan a bit lower. Does your own moan turn you on?

Sigh

There are literally thousands of possible tones to a sigh. How is your sigh? Is it deep and relaxed? Does it say, "I feel great"? Does it say, "Do it more"? Does it say, "Yes, yes, yes"?

Growl

Yes, growl. Let the animal in you escape and propel you to wilder and more carnal experiences. Send out a message with your growl. What does it say? Practice until you have several various growls stating pleasure, need, completion, primitive and uncivilized passion.

Purr

Imagine the first touch, the first lick, the first moment when you begin the voyage to passion and pleasure. How good it is. What fabulous expectations. What exquisite moments to come. Purr to express the feelings within your body. Say it with a purr. "Ohhhh yes, what a time we're having."

Squeal

There are moments when nothing expresses the feeling like a squeal. The touch so incendiary, the flame so hot, the feeling needs a totally infantile and uninhibited sound—a squeal. When did your body feel the need to release with a squeal? Try it now, it's regressive, infantile, and indescribably delicious.

Scream

There are orgasms, promises, moments of such intensity that only a scream can express the feeling. Try to scream without the high pitch or unpleasantness often associated with screams. Screams have a bad reputation because too often there is a discordant quality to screams. She may be in the throes of ecstasy and release a scream that, unfortunately, pierces his eardrum or is so unpleasant a pitch as to turn him off. I know it is difficult to control your sounds when passion is the impetus and the mind has nothing to do with your behavior. Practicing a scream can help to tone it down and make it a turn-on all of the time. Scream from your belly, not your throat. Scream with joy and appreciation. Scream whenever you feel it, and remember that you're lucky to feel it, so don't hold back—let it go.

Shout

It is more common for men to shout than women. The shout is a deep-throated scream, but is usually vocalized for the same motivations as the scream. There are Whoopees and Wohohos. There are Whoopdedoos, Howdydoodees, as well as Me Tarzans. Shouts are music to our ears because they tell us how magnificent and fabulous the moment is. So shout to let your partner know exactly how wonderful you feel.

Deep Breathing

The sounds of breath entering the lungs and leaving the lungs are very stimulating. The air entering and exiting, again and again, is relaxing. The slow, deep, breathy sound is not only a turn-on to your partner, it is a turn-on to you as well. Deep breathing is so relaxing that the entire body responds with an intensified sensitivity. When you breathe deeply, you can concentrate on the touch, the feel, and the smell of sex. Deep breathing and the breathy sounds of it enhance and provoke deeper feelings and more intensified passion. Breathe deeply into your genitals. Watch the breath stimulate your erogenous areas. Use your breath for enhancing the pleasure for both of you.

Hum

Put your lips against an ear, a nipple, a labia, or a penis and hum. The vibrations from your mouth will stir the juices and the sounds of the hum will stir the brain (our most powerful sex organ). Hum into a belly button or an anus. Hum under the arm, or inside the elbow or knee. Hum loud and long, and watch the blood stir and the flames ignite.

Laughter

Yes, I know laughter is very tricky. If it's at the wrong time, in the wrong tone, or for the wrong reason, it can be disastrous. But laughter to express delight, to express fun, to express how joyful you are feeling is not only a compliment, it is an affirmation of the happiness you experience with each other. Laugh. It feels good and it conveys a very positive message.

Silence

The sounds of silence are often as powerful as the sounds of sex. There are moments so intense, so stirring, when the body is so sensitized and highly charged, you can only be silent. You are merged with each other in a connection so deep, there is no consciousness, no thought, no sound. There is only the physical—the flow of blood, the beating of hearts, the tingling of skin. There is only the sexual expression of your bodies, entwined and seamlessly connected. There is silence. And then there is release with the sounds of sex, a harmony of sounds.

The Words She Loves to Hear

I asked one hundred women what words or expressions they love to hear when they are making love. The following are their responses. Are your favorite expressions included? If not, what are they? Add your own favorites before you share the list with your lover.

I love you. • I love touching you. • You are so beautiful. • I love your body. • I need you. • I love kissing you. • I can't wait. • I've been dreaming of this all day. • Do it to me. • Give me more. • You are so hot. • I can't stop touching you. • I never get enough of you.

She loves "dirty" talk too:

Your cunt is sooo hot. • I love how juicy you are. • Your cunt is delicious. • I love eating you. • I want to suck your tits. • Your tits are gorgeous. • Your tits are delicious. • I love fucking you. • Give me more juice. • I want to make you cum again and again. • I love how you suck. • I love what you're doing. • I love your ass.

Do these words turn you on? Would you like your man to say these things to you while making love? What else would you like to hear? Share your likes and dislikes with your lover.

The Words He Loves to Hear

You drive me crazy. • I'm cummming, I'm cummming. • Fuck me. • Suck me. • I love your body. • What a great ass.

• It's sooo goood. • Give it to me. • Now, baby, now. • Take me. • I'm all yours. • You do me so good. • I want you so much. • You fill me up. • You are so hard. • You are so delicious. • Kiss me. • Lick my tits. • Here they are, all yours. • Here I am, all yours. • Do it baby, do it. • Give me the slide. • Give me the up-top. • Give me the ride. • Give me the hop-hop. • Give me the roll-a-round. • Give me the big lick. • Give me the big boy.

Many men I spoke with really get turned on when their sexual techniques are given nicknames such as these. Use your imagination as to what these mean and pick your own names for your various favorite positions and techniques. You'll enjoy asking for these "specials" with a breathy, needy, urgent sound.

What We Don't Want to Hear

You're The Best!

What's wrong with this? Everyone wants to be the best. But when you're making love there is a danger of feeling that you are being compared to someone else. Even though the comparison is favorable, it still can be troubling and that's not what you want.

Try saying something like:

"You make me happier and happier," or,

"Every loving moment with you is better and better," or

"I love how excited you get me. You get me crazier and crazier every time."

In other words, your comparisons and compliments are based exclusively on the lover you are with at the moment, without a remote possibility that your words reflect another lover or another experience.

I Don't Like It.

Oh, no. Please don't tell your lover you don't like something, certainly not when you're in the throes of passion. Imagine being in a state of absolute ecstasy and fire and you hear the insulting words, "I don't like that." What a come down. Of course if you don't like something, tell your lover about it at an appropriate time. Discuss it during one of your discussions out of the bedroom, when you have a contract to discuss an important issue, and when you are both agreeing to be respectful and loving, not angry and hurtful.

"I don't like that," when expressed in the heat of the moment, is denigrating and very disrespectful. If your lover is trying to please you, accept it for the moment. If a touch or a movement or a behavior is so distasteful to you that you truly can't abide it, try a distraction—move your body a bit, begin to kiss lips, or stroke hair, or massage the neck. Do whatever is necessary, but *don't* say you don't like it.

Do It This Way!

When you're in the moment, remember the subtleties of sex talk before you begin issuing instructions. If you want her to suck harder, don't just say, "Harder, harder." You might whisper, in a breathy, deep voice, "I love how hard you suck me." This is both a compliment and a challenge. She will, of course, want to suck even harder when you tell her how much you love her hard sucking. If you want him to go faster, use the same technique. In a passionate voice with a seductive tone, tell him how much you love how hard he is and how fast and hard he fucks you. You may say, "I love your hard cock, I love your fast cock, I love you."

These are very touchy moments. On one hand, you want it the way you want it, when you want it. On the other hand, you don't want to demean or insult or turn off your lover. Be sensitive. Don't give orders. It is best to suggest, imply, challenge, tease, seduce, and succeed. You may want to be subtle and move your own body more quickly, or closer, or away, or whatever it takes to put yourself in the position you want. You may want to move his hand, or her leg, or your face. Be loving and respectful at all times. Be hot and horny and needy, but don't be demanding or authoritative. Be giving and responsive and passionate and watch your satisfaction soar.

Asking

It almost goes without saying that you should never ask questions such as: "Did you like it?" "Was it good for you?" "Did the earth move?" "Was I the best?" "Am I a good lover?" It is a turn-off for many reasons. First of all, it is true that if you have to ask, maybe it wasn't very good. When passion is glorious and electrifying and earth-rockingly magnificent, you don't have to ask. You *know* it, you *feel* it.

When you are secure as a lover, it manifests itself in how you make love and in how satisfying the lovemaking is for both of you. If you are secure in this you never ask. If you are insecure, you always ask. Become more secure with the ideas and techniques in sex talk. Become more secure within yourself as you enjoy and pleasure and excite yourself and your lover. Become more aware of the do's and the don'ts, and you won't have to ask.

This is also true of silly questions like: "Did I take care of you?" "Am I a good Mommy?" "Am I a good Daddy?" "Did I feed my baby goooood?" "Does my baby feel good?" This type of question only serves to separate you from your real identity. You are not a daddy or a mommy or a baby. The experience is of two adults, not of an infantilized man and woman. Use your own names and your own identities, not a false veil to mask your own fears or insecurities or embarrassment. Of course, you may have nicknames for each other. It is a fact that the more nicknames we have, the closer and more loving we seem to be. But, unless mommy or daddy or baby are your special private names, you're better off leaving them alone.

I'm Not In the Mood, I Changed My Mind.

Imagine being in the arms of your lover. You're kissing, you're touching, your juices are flowing, and you hear, "I'm not in the mood." Nobody wants to hear these words. I suggest that, even if you're truly *not* in the mood, you don't say a word. Your body will take over if you allow it. Let the touching, kissing, and caressing *put* you in the mood. Remember that passion and sexual desire is a physiological response to a variety of cues. Allow the stimulation to turn you on, and your "bad mood" may very well be turned off. If you suddenly think of a chore you need to do, or a word he said that you didn't like, or that she insulted your mother this afternoon, your response may be to withdraw. But don't do it. Pouring cold water on your hot body would be less painful than hearing, "I'm not in the mood."

What is it that *you* don't want to hear? What words or sounds or behaviors are painful to you? Share helpful suggestions when the timing, the agreement, and the situation are appropriate. When you are having a cup of coffee, touching each other's hands, looking into each other's eyes, and agreeing to discuss these issues, talk about it. Tell your lover what she said that you felt badly about. Tell your lover what he said that hurt your feelings. It is best to discuss these issues some place other than in bed, and certainly some time other than when the heat of passion is making you vulnerable. Share your thoughts with your lover at an appropriate moment, not during your lovemaking or during a sensitive moment.

Sounds and words are reflective of our feelings, needs, and satisfactions. Sounds and words enhance the moment. You create sensations and motivations that would not be experienced without sounds and words. Sex talk is a turn-on because the body actually does respond physiologically, not just emotionally. Sex talk is a turn-on because the mind needs the reassurance, impetus, and motivation to perpetuate passion and lust.

Sex talk is a necessity for all of these reasons, and because it is fun. Sounds and words are exciting and pleasurable and fun. Sex talk is a necessity because we are thinking, feeling, intelligent humans who use language to express ourselves. What better way to create the sensations we want and need and enjoy than to express these feelings with words and sounds? Don't miss out on the treasure chest within your voice box. Use the words and the sounds that will get you what you want, when you want it, and how you want it. Use sex talk with love and respect and joy. The benefits are all yours.

chapter 7

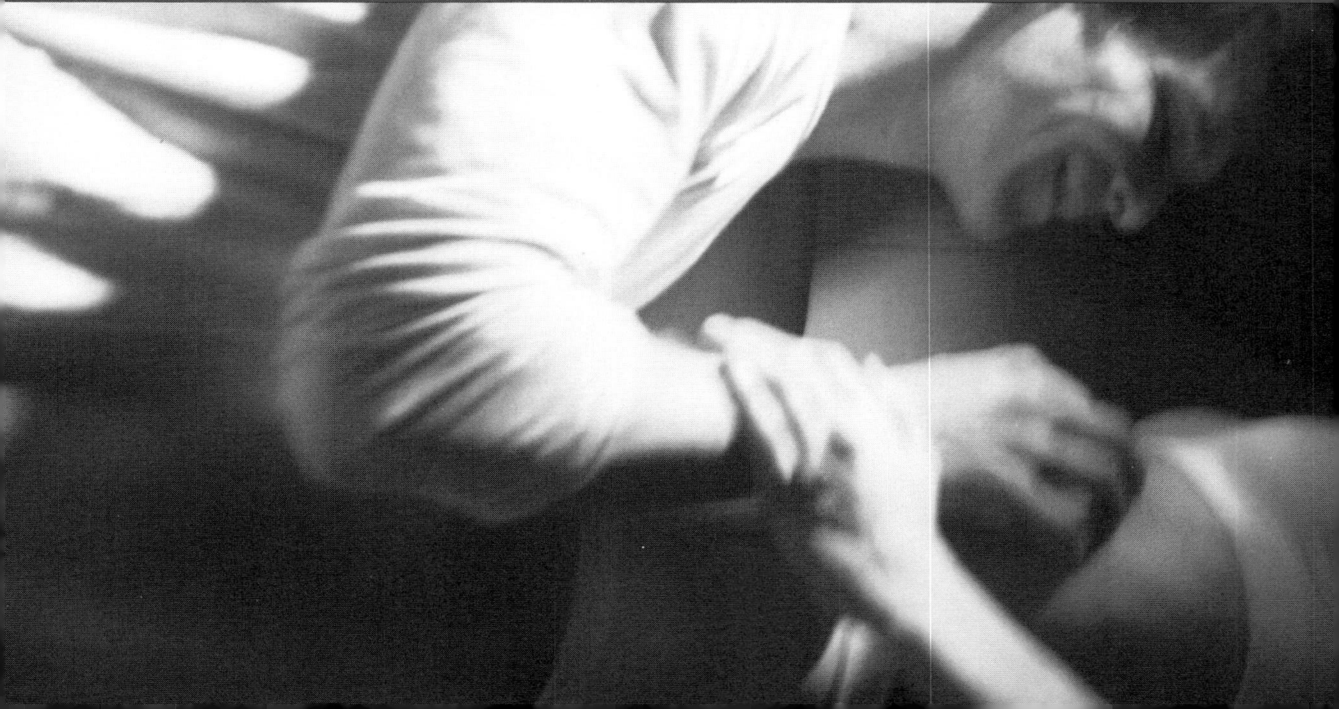

sex games for fun, stimulation, and pleasure

Remember when you were six years old and you bounced from bed to bed, throwing pillows and laughing hysterically? Remember how you rolled from side to side, shivering with delight, gleefully hugging your mother or father or sister or brother or friend? Remember those moments of pure abandonment, without thought or goal, without worry or expectation? Think about how glorious it could be if you returned to such moments with an open heart, an open mind, and an open body. Imagine the unbridled passion that could be unleashed by including laughter and fun in your lovemaking.

These are games that have been played successfully and joyfully by thousands of couples. Try the ones that appeal to you. Try the ones that seem foolish, even ridiculous. Even if a game idea turns you off, try it. You may discover a source of exhilaration and freedom you never knew you could enjoy. You may notice that if you do feel turned off, it is merely a defense mechanism, a barrier to possible pleasure. Try all of these games. You just might discover a moment of joyous release as you experience the laughing and the playing, in an atmosphere of unbridled surrender.

Please remember, although you will be asking for certain behaviors, modifying requests and techniques, there is no place for a demeaning or critical manner. As in all games, there are rules, and as you follow the rules, you will discover the benefits. The rules are for both of you, not against either one.

Sexual pleasure as well as sexual play is limited only by the scope of your imagination. Your mind is your most powerful sex organ. It is your mind that can open the door to pleasure, excitement, and laughter. Allow yourself the freedom to be the child who rolled in the grass, dove through the waves, and jumped up and down on the bed. Let go. Be silly. Be happy. Have fun!

Game # 1. Do My Spots

As with all of the suggestions in *Sex Talk*, begin by agreeing that you're doing this for fun. Any instruction or request is to increase the fun and keep the game fast paced. Of course, the game portion will end eventually and passion will take over. But during the game instructions will fly and requests will be made. It's all part of the game.

You will need: Post-It Notes. A pen. Two nude bodies.

Decide on a fun penalty in case you are not satisfied with the way the game is being played. The penalty can be whatever you dream up and can be imposed at any time. You may demand a long, one-minute kiss, a spanking with a feather, or a dish of whipped cream to be eaten from a body part. The penalty is designed to add more fun and imagination to the game.

Take turns playing this game. Take turns placing post-its on your favorite body parts. For example, she may number her breasts *l*, and her vagina *2*. He may number his penis *l* and his testicles *2*.

Once you've placed the Post-It Notes where you want them, your partner proceeds to lavish attention on the numbered parts in the designated order. Or, you can call out the number of the spot you want attended to. He may begin kissing one spot, but you may want him rubbing another. She may begin to lick your number five spot, but you may prefer that a different spot be licked or stroked. Call out the number of the area you want "done." Call out the type of stimulation you want at that spot. Change places as often as you'd like. Continue until you have both reached *all* of the spots, or until your body is demanding more serious sexual "play."

You will find that the more you instruct, the more often you change direction, the more often you *do not* follow instructions or *do not* comply, the more fun you will have. The goal is *not* serious lovemaking. It is true that the fun is likely to turn into even more highly charged sexual pleasuring, but don't be in a hurry.

If you've chosen a penalty, you may call for it at any time. You impose this penalty if your partner does not follow instructions, or if they do not pay attention in the order you require, or if they do not kiss or lick or stroke as advised. (Remember, half the fun is being silly.) The agreement is that they accept and perform the penalty immediately.

Game # 2. Under the Hole

You will need: A sheet, large towel, or pillowcase with a hole cut in the center of the fabric. A blindfold. You may also want to have some massage oils, ice cubes, feathers, velvet, satin, aromatics, or other stimulating materials available.

Begin by agreeing to have fun with this game. Decide who will go first. Lie down with your entire body covered with the fabric. Position the hole in the fabric so that you expose just one body part. Put on the blindfold so that whatever is being done to your spot will remain a surprise and an adventure until you feel it, rather than see it. You will also be surprised at how much more exciting it will be when you are blindfolded.

Your partner then proceeds to attend to the exposed body part in whatever way he or she would like. You may begin to lick or suck or stroke or knead. You may use oils, or stroke with a feather or piece of satin. You may use sounds or aromas or whatever your imagination conjures. Ice cubes are very stimulating on the erogenous zones as is a light feather stroke or a "satin rub." The entire body will be on high alert. Whichever body part is exposed, and whatever stimulation is given to that spot, will be felt with fierce sensitivity.

The blindfolded partner chooses the first spot he/she wants to expose. After that the "doer" chooses the spots to expose. Change the spot often, change the type of stimulation often. Give yourself time to have fun with it before the passion takes over. Be whimsical and silly with the stimulations you choose or the game may end too early. If at first you are too sexual or too passionate, within minutes you may be highly charged and crying for more. Of course, at some point, the game will end, giving way to the sexual satisfaction inspired by the game.

Game # 3. A Variation on Spin the Bottle

You will need: A bottle of course. Any sexy props you may want to use, such as those suggested for the Under The Hole game.

As always, the rules are to have fun, not be insulted by instructions or requests, and be respectful of each other. You can play this game either clothed or nude. If you choose to wear clothing, undressing your partner will be part of the game.

Lie on your side facing your partner. Place the bottle near your partner, at about the center of his/her body. Spin the bottle. Wherever the bottle points is the spot that gets the attention. Do whatever pleases you to that spot. You may want to use a feather or some oil. You may want to spritz it with perfume or plain water. You may want to place your lips on the spot and hum into it. You may want to insert something into the spot, or taste the spot. You may want to blow on the spot and kiss the spot. The choices are limitless.

The one receiving the attention can call out "change" at any time that you would like the spot to be changed. Or you can call out "no" if you don't like what is being done to the spot. Spin the bottle again to discover a new spot.

Game # 4. Hide and Seek (Or Seek and Do)
In this game, a variation on the childhood game of hide and seek, you will hide an item that you want your partner to use, or that you want to use on your partner. For example, she may hide a vibrator because she wants to him to stimulate her with it. If he finds it, he has the power to use it as he

wants to. If he wants a massage, he may hide some massage oil. If she finds it, she can use the oil as she wishes.

You could hide peanut butter because you want it eaten from your body. Or bath oil because you'd love to take a sexy bath together. You may want to hide shampoo so that he can wash your hair, or shaving cream so that she can shave you.

This game is a doorway to satisfying a fantasy. Hide the item that you've always wanted to enjoy. Hide edible panties, or a dildo, or handcuffs, or a turn-on film or magazine. Hide an outfit you'd like her to tease you with or a mask you'd like him to put on. Your imagination has no boundaries—let it go, let it fly. Use this game as an opportunity to express yourself.

Game # 5. Mirroring

In this game, you both agree to follow the movements and behaviors of your partner. If he moves one way, you will move in the same way. If she licks a particular spot, you will lick the analogous spot on her.

Begin without touching each other. It is fun to make eye contact and watch each other closely. Raise your arms and slowly sway from side to side. Your partner will mirror your movements by swaying side to side as well. Continue this non-touching mirroring. Make faces, reach up, reach down, turn, dance, walk on toes, walk on hands and knees, etc.

As you become tuned in to each other, following fluidly and rhythmically, you will become very sensitive to each other's moods and movements. Be sure to do this slowly and for at least five minutes so that you really become aligned with each other.

When you are truly moving as one, begin to touch each other. Touch an arm, a nose, a mouth. Each touch will be mirrored as slowly and as tenderly as possible. Mirror the movement in as similar a manner as possible. Be as soft, as tender, as loving in your connections to each other.

Begin to kiss body parts, to stimulate erogenous areas, to become more and more sexual in the mirroring. A lick on the nose begets a lick on the nose. A sucking of a finger begets a sucking of a finger. As you intensify and become more and more sexual in your connections, the electricity will be on high wattage and your nerve endings will be howling for release.

This is the perfect opportunity to touch yourself where and how you want to be touched. As he/she mirrors what you are doing, they will become aware of what you like and how you like it. When the game turns to lovemaking, you will both incorporate what you've learned from the mirroring game.

Game # 6. Tit for Tat

Make a list of all the things you'd like from your partner. This game is not only fun, it is extremely informative. Because it's a game, you are free to ask for anything you've been wanting, but have not yet expressed. You will also become very adept at negotiating and satisfying each other's needs.

You may list a romantic dinner, a full body massage, an hour of kissing, a slave for a week, and so on. List whatever you would like and share your lists. As you read your partner's list, put check marks on the items you are willing to do. You may put numbers next to the items in the order in which you would like to comply. You may choose to comply with the request for a body scrub first, and a one-hour massage second.

What you include in your list is entirely up to you. You are also in control of which requests you will comply with. Remember, you will be in agreement as to what you are receiving in return. Decide what you will do in return for something on your partner's list. For example, you agree to give a one-hour massage if she will agree to ten minutes of fellatio. Or she agrees to give you twenty-four hours of total subservience if you give her the romantic dinner and dancing she's listed. This is a perfect way to practice your negotiation skills and your ability to cooperate with each other.

Enjoy the game, laugh at the silly requests, and compliment the excellent ideas you share with each other. Learn as much as you can about each other's needs and wants. This is a perfect opportunity to share a fetish or fantasy. You may request that your partner wear stockings while making love, or that he wear a long blonde wig. Open yourselves and your secret desires in an atmosphere of fun and sharing. Enhance and develop your love and your enjoyment by sharing and satisfying as much as possible.

Game # 7. The Power of Body Parts

We have certain abilities inherent in our various body parts. We can do a great deal with our bodies, and too often we restrict ourselves from utilizing the full scope of our proficiency.

This game will stimulate you to think of new and exciting ways to use your body so that sexual pleasures are constantly being developed and improved. It is fun to be imaginative and to try out all of the ideas you may have been harboring, but never articulated.

As you think of what you can do with various body parts, and begin to list these behaviors, remember this is a list of what *you* can do with each particular body part to please your partner. This is not a list of what you want done to *your* body part.

For example you may list that you can use your fingers to stimulate an erogenous area, or you can use your hands to give a massage, or you can use your palms to cup her breasts, or his testicles. You may write that you can use your tongue to trace the curves of her nose or lips. You may write that you can use your teeth to scratch an itch or stimulate a nipple.

Use your imagination. Think outside the box as far as you can. Create new motions and actions and behaviors that will please, stimulate, satisfy, seduce, and arouse.

Body Parts Game Contract

- For every original and unique technique you write that is not included on my list, I will give you a treat of your choice.
- I agree to engage in the fun and adventure of actually performing the techniques I write on my list. I also agree to enjoy the pleasures of what you write on your list.

Body Parts Game Rules

- Body parts are listed individually so that you will concentrate on the particular and extensive possibilities for each part.
- Write or verbally share as many actions as you can imagine with each part listed.
- If you are especially interested in a particular action, practice it whenever you'd like. Consider all ideas presented and try them out.

A. What can I do with my hands?

This includes your fingers, your fist, your palm, your knuckles, etc. Make a list of everything that you can do with your hands. Consider what you can do with your hands to have fun with each other, and what you can do to sexually please your partner.

B. What can I do with my mouth?

This includes every part of the mouth—lips, tongue, teeth, breath, sounds, etc. Consider what you can do with your mouth to have fun with each other, and what you can do to sexually please your partner.

C. What can I do with my legs?

This includes knees, ankles, toes, thighs, etc. Consider what you can do with your legs to have fun with each other, and what you can do to sexually please your partner.

D. What can I do with my breasts?

Consider what you can with your breasts (men have breasts, too) to have fun with each other, and what you can do to sexually please your partner.

E. What can I do with my full body?

Consider what you can do with your full body to have fun with each other, and what you can do to sexually please your partner.

F. What can I do with my vagina?

This includes labia, clitoris, vaginal cavity, pubic hair, etc. Consider what you can do with your vagina to have fun with each other, and what you can do to sexually please your partner.

G. What can I do with my penis?

This includes the penis and testicles. Consider what you can do with your penis to have fun with each other, and what you can do to sexually please your partner.

Sharing your imaginative, fun, and enticing ideas by both discussing and performing them is not only informative, it can be incredibly funny as well as sexually exciting. Writing and discussing these things will also stimulate your imagination and open the doors to new, provocative, and exhilarating behaviors.

Playing sex games is one modality that you can use to open yourselves to the fantastic and exhilarating world of sexual enhancement. You won't know how far your imagination will take you, or how much you can add to your sexual pleasure, until you start to play with it. Trust the process, and each other. The fun you have and the discoveries you make are limited only by your imagination—and your flexibility.

Sexual game playing is a universe unto itself. There are certainly requirements, such as love and respect and a joyful sense of your lives together. You will "play" and enjoy the games more often if you realize that all relationships benefit from laughter and lighthearted connections. The deep, passionate connections we need are enhanced by laughter. You will be amazed at how much you will learn about each other and how beneficial these games will be to your relationship.

What games would you like to play? Are there some that you can devise which will bring you closer, create the fun and laughter so important to the enhancement of love? Think about what you'd like to play. Think about what you can offer each other as you play sexual games.

chapter 8

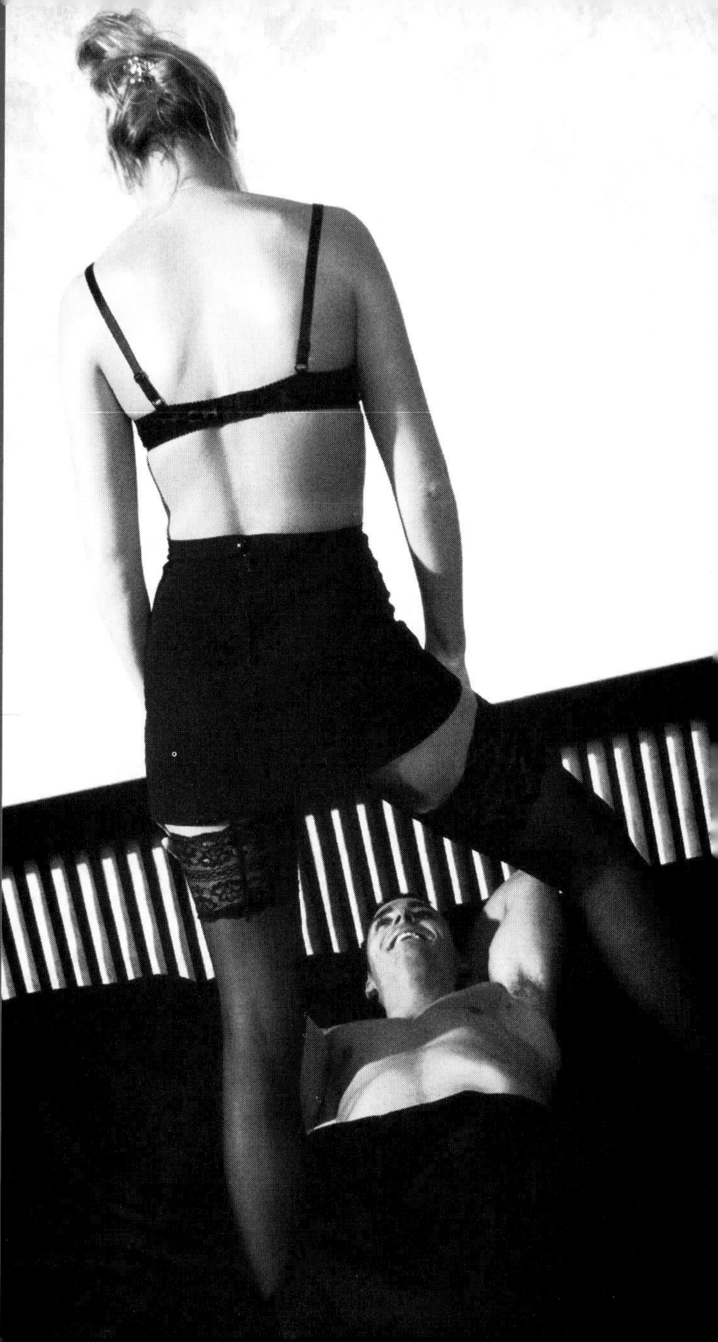

the pleasure
of fantasies

Fantasy brings brightness and color to your life. It is with imagination, adventure, exploration, and discovery that we increase the excitement in our lives. It is with fantasy that we ignite moments with exhilaration and fulfillment. It is with fantasy that we keep the boring and uneventful away from our door. If you open yourself to the joys of your fantasies, you will float along the rainbow of color and light to the legendary and elusive pot of gold. Allowing your fantasies to roam freely, without restrictions or judgments, is your key to a more thrilling and varied life—sexually, intellectually, and emotionally.

A fantasy is a dream, a hope, an escape to incredible joy. It is also, of course, an excellent access to enhanced and intensified pleasure. Our brain is our most powerful sexual organ, and it is our brain that fantasizes. It follows, therefore, that fantasy is a source of increasing sexual pleasure. If you open yourself to your fantasies, you will feel your spirits soar and your levels of pleasure explode with incredible passion.

Fantasy works. It increases your libido, it pumps up your energy, it stimulates the blood flow, and most importantly, it gives you the impetus to behave in ways that will satisfy the fantasy. It has been scientifically proven that our immune system is strengthened dramatically when we are happy and joyous. It also improves when we are in love. A recent research project proved that our immune system improves just as dramatically when we "fantasize" that we are in love. Participants in the study were wired so that their physiological responses could be recorded. They were asked to think about the person they loved, and to imagine that they were on their way to a romantic meeting. Another group, comprised of people without partners, was asked to do the same. They fantasized that they were in love and fantasized about a romantic meeting with an imaginary partner. The results were surprising. Measures of their immune system, blood pressure, acidity, and muscle tension showed marked physiological improvements. Whether the thoughts were real or fantasized, the health benefits were exactly the same.

Sadly, most people have developed obstacles to encouraging their fantasies; impediments that control behavior and are often destructive. We create and perpetuate obstacles out of childhood restrictions, emotional vulnerability, and distorted opinions of right and wrong. These obstacles keep us from sharing our fantasies or even allowing our fantasies to develop. They remain in the dark recesses, never to take flight, never to carry us to lofty heights of pleasure.

The word fantasy has somehow taken on a pejorative meaning. If we discuss our imagination, we are rewarded and commended. But if we use the word fantasy, we are looked upon as childish or immature, even emotionally disturbed. So we nurture our fantasies deep within ourselves, never to be shared or explored.

Why are we so often reluctant to share our fantasies with our partners? For one thing, we don't want to discuss fantasies about other partners for fear of inciting jealousy and anger. Although a fantasy about making love to a movie star, war hero, or historical figure is absolutely unachievable, we don't share this fantasy for fear of hurting feelings.

One night while watching Julio Iglesias perform at a Las Vegas casino, a woman at my table sighed and murmured that Julio was "quite a hunk." Her husband became so angry that he left the table. Why was he so upset? Her "fantasy" about Julio could have been explored to bring passion to the highest peak for both of them. It would be the husband who would benefit, not the celebrity. So why did he deprive himself and his wife of what could have been a fabulously exciting night?

He felt threatened and deprived of the exclusive attention of his wife. He felt inadequate because his wife was "turned on" by another man. Then he felt foolish and immature, and was too embarrassed to return to the table, therefore missing most of the show. Unfortunately, this kind of unproductive behavior is not uncommon.

Since a fantasy often includes a person or situation outside the relationship, you may become frightened or insecure, feeling that an outside source of excitement should not be necessary, that if your relationship were all it should be you *wouldn't need* to fantasize. But if we can embellish and improve our experience of life, excite and seduce ourselves to higher passion and greater fulfillment, then why not do it in whatever way we can?

Ninety percent of men and 75 percent of women have fantasies that do not include their lover. A man can visualize a certain woman or even a body part and become immediately aroused. A woman can think of a scenario that excites her and use the scenario to improve her sexual experience. Fantasy is proven to be extremely conducive to enhancing sexual experience, even when it is kept secret. It is much more exciting and much more fulfilling if the fantasy can be shared. How can we accomplish this? How can we get beyond the fear of failure or ridicule? How can we avoid hurting each other or creating an abyss of pain and anger between each other?

Sex talk with respect and love can accomplish anything. Believe that, and be open about what you want and need. Try this simple experiment: Walk around the room as yourself for just a minute. How did you feel? How did you look? Now walk around the room as Albert Einstein, or Winston Churchill, or someone who you admire very much. How did you feel? How did you look? It is usually true that on the second walk your shoulders are more squared, your head higher, and your step springier.

Now try this. Suck on your finger as though you were sucking and licking a body part of your partner. Now pretend to be the movie star of your dreams, the idol of your fantasies. Suck on the same body part as though you were the star. How was it different? Usually, the experience, although just a personal fantasy, it is more exciting and more creative. Was this true for you?

Sometimes we hesitate to discuss fantasies we suspect are strange or weird for fear of being judged and rejected, even though we know that a fantasy is an imaginary situation and probably impossible to achieve. But it is worth the risk because the results can be so rewarding for yourself and your partner. Consider your fantasies as explorations into a wilder, more exciting, more passionate relationship. If you accept the benefits and the excitement of your fantasies, you might be more willing to explore them. It is possible to share fantasies without the risk of rejection or shame.

When you introduce fantasy, there are precautions to be aware of and many possible avenues to travel. You may fear disrupting the status quo, hurting your lover's feelings, damaging their self-esteem, or creating a vacuum of intimacy because you include an image outside the relationship. Realize that your partner may be defensive and self-protective. Be sensitive about threatening or actually hurting your partner if you share a fantasy that does not include him or her. There are, I know, some fantasies you may not want to share, yet if you look at them closely, you can ask yourself why not?

Following is a simple game you can play to get you started. In the first game, your partner decides who he/she wants you to be for the moment. If she says she loves Harrison Ford, he asks her, "If I were Harrison Ford, what would you like me to do to you now?"

The second half of this game is to switch. She asks whom he would love to make love to. He chooses whom he loves and she behaves as he would like his choice to behave. If he says Julia Roberts, she asks him what he would like Julia Roberts to do to him now.

It is amazing to watch the change in the persona when you take on the role of another person. It is also fun and exciting to be "done to" by the character being played. When wearing the mask of a "star," inhibitions are released, responsibility is erased, and adventure becomes limitless.

Or, you may say, "I'd love you to pretend to be (add whoever it is that you fantasize about) and do what you would do if you were him or her." This slight switch in the game is an easy segue into fulfilling your fantasy without hurting or threatening. It is all in fun, and the fun will be worth the effort.

There are thousands of fantasies that do not include a particular person or memory. There are fantasies of character types, such as nurses or doctors, as well as fantasies that center around certain places, animals, or fabrics.

The predominant fantasy of many women is bondage and domination. This has nothing to do with rape or unwanted sexual contact. It is the feeling of being without power and without responsibility, therefore without blame or consequence. Women love the feeling that they can be wild and impulsive, highly sexual and passionate without any responsibility for their actions. If he "takes" her, she is without control, without culpability. She can let go and be totally responsive. All of the early childhood training of "don't" and "careful" and how ladies are supposed to act can be washed away because he is doing it, not her.

Women love to be needed and wanted so deeply that the man has no restraint, no delayed gratification, no ability to resist. Her man acts as though he cannot be without her for even one more second. He takes her then and there, and she revels in the unmistakable desire and power he manifests.

If a woman asks for this from her lover, it is not as fulfilling or exciting. It becomes contrived and pales in comparison to the spontaneous and uncontrolled act she fantasizes about. But if a man knows that this is one of the most common fantasies of women, he may act on it occasionally and impulsively.

Some of the women I interviewed shared these moments with me:

"We were visiting a friend in the hospital when Mark pulled me into an empty room, pushed me on the bed, pulled my pantyhose down and, before I knew what was happening, he was inside of me. I was holding the pillow against my face to keep in the moaning and groaning provoked by my orgasmic release. He kept saying he couldn't help himself, he just had to do it, he needed me right then and there. I loved him and the sex and especially how he glowed as we discreetly left the room."

"We were in St. Johns the Divine Church in Manhattan and wandered into a small, seemingly private prayer room. It was very dimly lit and we knelt on the red satin pillows meant for prayer. The quiet, the spiritualism, the beauty of the room was creating a sense of deep peacefulness in me, when Steve suddenly pulled me to him and began kissing me with such fervor, I was at first surprised and then I was, as they say in the movies, swept away.

"We made love there in the church on the red satin pillows and I will never forget the connection that we felt. Steve tried to apologize later, saying he was embarrassed because it was probably blasphemous to have done what we did. I told him I was sure that God would appreciate and applaud the joy and love that we shared, because I certainly did. It was wonderful."

"We were on the beach, lying on a blanket and just touching each other's fingers. We were relaxed in the sun and tired from our long swim. Jim sat up very suddenly and pulled me onto his lap. The beach was crowded and I was a bit surprised at how he was kissing me in front of all the people. He pulled my bathing suit aside and suddenly he was inside me. We barely moved, appearing to be a couple just kissing as I sat on his lap. I prayed that they couldn't see anything else. Then, I stopped thinking about anyone or anything except the feeling of his penis inside me. He pulled his penis up and down, but didn't move his body at all. The slow movements inside me were invisible to the rest of the world, but I could feel every sensation. He kept kissing me. My orgasm was so explosive that I couldn't help the noises that came from me. Jim kept his mouth on mine so they were barely audible. I loved what he did. I loved that he wanted me that minute and showed it. I'm glad we didn't get arrested, though."

Paula told me that one of her most exciting moments was during a vacation in Hawaii. She said:

"We were walking through the lobby of the hotel when Don slowed his pace and began walking behind me. He whispered into my ear that he wanted me to go into our room and lie naked on the bed with a blindfold on. He instructed me to spread my arms and legs, lie on my back and not move. He said he would follow me in a few minutes and that I should wait for him. He also said that I should lie perfectly still, regardless of what he did to me. He asked me to agree to all of his directions. I did, and I will tell you that the entire time I was undressing, putting stockings over my eyes as a blindfold, and waiting nude and spread-eagled on the bed, was one of the most thrilling times of my sexual life.

"When he arrived it was even better."

How can a female tell her partner that she dreams of such moments? An excellent style is to share information that is statistically significant—about other people.

If a man learns of the most predominant fantasy of "other" women, he may realize it is a good idea to act on this every once in a while. If he reads about these fantasies and his woman agrees that this type of behavior does excite her, he may act on it spontaneously.

It is true for men as well. Men love to have their woman be the aggressor. It is thrilling to have your penis stroked during a dinner party, or be followed into the men's room so that she can lick and taste a certain body part. He will explode with passion if you include these behaviors every once in a while.

Jay shared his most passionate moment and was happy to say that Dale has repeated this from time to time. He told me, "The first time it happened, we were on a cruise and we were dancing. I had an erection, which Dale could feel. She danced me out of the room, out a door, and out on the deck. She unzipped my pants and began to suck on me, there on her knees, in the moonlight, on the deck, unaware and unconcerned if anyone else was around. I actually exploded in two seconds, it was so exciting. She's repeated this several times on different occasions. Each and every time it's a fabulous surprise and wow, it's a knockout of pleasure."

Barry and Shari told me of a similar situation. Shari said, "Sometimes when Barry and I are out with other couples, I can see that he is tired or really not interested. I know that he'd rather be home watching TV or playing video games. So I decided to make our nights out a bit more exciting for him, giving him something to hope for and anticipate.

"I lean over and whisper some outrageous sexual pleasure I intend to explore as soon as we get home. I grab his ass and his penis and his balls as often as I can, under the table, while we're walking, whenever. I also lean over and tease him with little licks and kisses on his penis as we're driving to and from wherever we're going. It makes our nights out more exciting for both of us."

Barry added that he never gets bored or tired or complains that he wants to go home because as he said, "I'm on pins and needles waiting for the next promise, or the next lascivious touch." He added, "Of course the ride home has lots of promise as well."

Be creative. Take charge. Do what you feel and what you know your partner will love. Enhance the passion and the desire with surprising and enticing behaviors. Tune in to each other and turn on as often as you can, as creatively as you can, and as wantonly as you can.

If your fantasy is to role-play a certain type of person, you may want to get the costume or style of dress of that type. For example, if you want to act like a hooker or a pimp during lovemaking, wear the appropriate attire. You could hide the outfit during a game of hide and seek (see Chapter 7), or you may just wear it as a surprise.

It is a good idea to share your thoughts before you put on the costume, just in case he is insulted that you want to be a hooker, or she feels offended by the behavior of a pimp. But, if you say, "How would you like me to be your slut, your whore, your private hooker," in a throaty, sexy, seductive voice as you stroke his ear and lick his face. It can be the carrot that you dangle before you act on the fantasy.

Once you're in the outfit, you will be surprised at how quickly and thoroughly you will take on the persona.

On the other hand, if he says he loves you the way you are and doesn't want you to be any other way, drop it. He is actually telling you that the idea is not pleasing to him. It is possible that some fantasies are offensive to others, so be sensitive to the reaction and don't be forceful. There's nothing wrong with the fantasy, it's just not working for your partner.

You can also act on your fantasy without the benefit of the appropriate outfit. You can be sluttish without stiletto heels, or dominating without black spike-heeled boots. You can, of course, wear "some" of your fantasy outfit, adding a bit at a time for your own pleasure, but without offending his sensitivity to the idea.

This is true of any of your fantasies about role-playing. Be a maid, a mother, a teacher, or a doctor. Be whomever you want to be as you make love. Start slowly and sensitively. Introduce the scenario with playfulness and a sense of adventure.

One man brought his son's blackboard into the bedroom. He began drawing stick figures and pointing to various body parts using a thick foreign accent. He playfully talked about the penis and the testicles saying these go together and need to be paid attention to. He said, "You take the balls here and put them here on top of the cock, you see, my little girl—you hold them together like this."

His wife laughed and admired his teaching role. She learned something he wanted done to him. She was aware that the game had a purpose and she responded to the lesson. He had always wanted to have his testicles and penis touched and stroked together. He wished his testicles were actually wrapped around his penis and that he could penetrate with the whole "package." His fantasy, played out as a teacher, accomplished the physical pleasure he fantasized about. She responded well because it was done in fun and playfulness, and not in a critical or demanding way.

They fulfilled his fantasy by having her hold his testicles tightly as he thrusts into her. During moreplay, she plays with him by wrapping his balls around his penis and massaging his penis with the flesh of his balls. The level of his passion has increased exponentially since they've added this technique, and he feels wildly satisfied.

One woman told me that she loved to pretend to be a wild animal, but was afraid to share it with her husband. She actually picked up men so that she could feel free to roll around on the bed growling and threatening with bared teeth and thrashing hands. Because she would never see these men again, she felt free to act on her fantasy without fear of rejection.

She began to feel very guilty about cheating, and tried to resist the compulsion she had to act like a wild animal during lovemaking. Unable to resolve her dilemma, she finally decided to take a risk and explore the possibility of sharing her need with her husband.

She tried the game of hide and seek, hiding a mask of a lion. They played with the mask for a while and when she put it on she was so incredibly turned on that she pleasured her husband as never before. He was so satiated that he suggested they use the mask *all* the time. Their lovemaking now includes growling and teeth baring, threatening with thrashing arms, and circling of her "prey." Their sexual pleasures have increased and she no longer has the need to explore this fantasy with other men.

There are many roads to any destination. If your fantasy is recurring, one that you really enjoy and would love to really experience, find a way to get there. Use a game, use a back door such as a teaching lesson, use teasing and seduction, but do try to be as fulfilled as possible. A fantasy need not be secret—it can become an experience of grand proportions.

Use the concepts I've described with the sensitivity of being totally respectful and totally responsive to the reactions of your partner. Use your imagination, remembering that your brain is your most powerful sexual organ. Use all of your skills to satisfy each and every one of your sexual needs. There is no doubt that your fantasies are absolutely valid sexual needs, which deserve to be satisfied.

enjoying a fetish

"The candlelight threw flickers of shadow and light on the ceiling, creating a romantic scenario. Ravel's 'Bolero' was playing and, as usual, I began to feel warm and excited. Larry was undulating his body towards me as he had so often in the past. He began thrusting forward and back, his pelvis moving to the rhythm, his ritual dance becoming more and more frenzied. Within a minute he was next to the bed and I turned to face him, my mouth on a level with his growing penis. He said the words he needed to say as he continued the movements he needed to make.

"'Open up baby, open up and let me in.' I took his penis into my mouth and kissed the head gently and lovingly. I began making love to my husband as he moved his body next to mine and responded to my loving with kisses and strokes of his own. The ritual was over and our lovemaking began, lovemaking that is as we dream about—lovemaking that is truly satiating and exciting, romantic and explosive. Larry and I love to make love, we just begin our loving differently than others do."

Perhaps Larry's ritual is strange by some standards, but for Penny it is the beginning of passionate and satisfying sex. If she didn't accept Larry's ritual, they would not enjoy the sexual pleasures they do. She is, therefore, more than happy to include it because it is what Larry needs.

Larry's "ritual" is known as a fetish, a psychological connection to an object, words, or behaviors that must be included in any sexual experience. For unknown reasons, women do not experience fetishes—it is an exclusively male phenomenon.

When he was a boy, Larry heard his father say, "Open up baby, open up and let me in." Ravel's "Bolero" was playing. As Larry listened he experienced his first climax. His nine-year-old penis became erect. He felt his body become tense and then release. He felt wetness and warmth and he felt wonderful. He lay in bed listening to sounds from his parents' bedroom that made him feel warm and tingly and safe. Larry became erotically attached to the words, the music, and the sensations. His erection became completely dependent on the memory of that moment. Without repeating the words, there was no erection for Larry. His fetish, his erotic connection, is to the words and the music. Since his body was moving in a thrusting motion as he lay on his bed listening, he has included these movements in his ritual.

Penny understands Larry's emotional connection to his ritual. She enjoys the pleasure they have with each other after he goes through his ritual. Most importantly, she understands that without the ritual there would be no love-making. She accepts it for their mutual benefit. After all, she told me, "It is very romantic—the music, the dance, the candles, and the sex. I love Larry and I really don't mind the few minutes he needs to 'get in the mood.' I actually like watching him, so why not enjoy it and not fight it? What would that get me?"

Thousands of women are responding to such questions with acceptance of their partner's sexual fetishes. A fetish is not a fantasy, a preference, a desire, or a wish. It is a need, which is so internalized, so fraught with emotional erotic connections, that sexual function is limited or even extinguished unless the fetish is satisfied and experienced.

Larry's is the type of fetish that is most appropriate for sex talk. His need is acceptable; one which can be gratified with an understanding partner. Larry shared his need with Penny very early in their relationship. At first he told her that he liked to perform, dancing and moving to music. Then he told her that he loved Ravel's "Bolero" and bought her a CD so that she could play it when they were together. The very first night that they made love, Larry danced for Penny and when he said the words, his penis at her mouth, it seemed very natural and loving. Penny responded with the passion of the moment.

Their lovemaking was wonderful and their relationship was growing into a deep and committed love. Larry told her that when they make love, he would *always* need to dance and to speak his ritualistic words. She accepted this because she loved him and because the results were always satisfying.

Some fetishists develop an exclusive or predominant sexual interest in an inanimate object or a part of the human body. The man may need to hold a pair of shoes or nylon stockings, wear spiked heels, look at a clock, wrap himself in satin, wear leather, suck on hair, wear underwear, and so on. The compulsive need for the object must be satisfied in order to achieve sexual satisfaction.

Rob is a perfect example of a man with a stocking fetish. When Rob was about three years old, he was sitting on the top step, able to see through the open door of the upstairs bathroom. He watched his mother's legs as she put on her stockings. At that moment, he became aware of an erection and the pleasure that the erection gave him. From that point on, Rob's turn-on cue for sexual arousal was a woman's legs in stockings. He loved stockinged legs and every woman he saw who was wearing stockings. If a ninety-year-old walked in front of him wearing stockings, he would feel a stir. He loved to shop for stockings, experiencing the warmth and pleasure of an erection and a feeling of love reminiscent of his love for his mother.

Joan accepted Rob's behavior because she loved him. Their lovemaking was very passionate. The fact that he held her stockinged legs, held stockings on his hands, and at times, even wore stockings himself, did not diminish the passion and the satisfaction she felt when they made love. In fact, Joan enjoyed doing a sexy show for Rob, slowly putting on stockings and showing her legs in a seductive manner.

Rob told Joan about his love of stockings on their very first date. She didn't think anything about it at first, but then began to question his "obsession" with stockings—his insisting that she wear them all the time, that she keep them on while they made love, and that he would wear them as well. He would sometimes rearrange her stocking drawer, saying it was fun for him to take care of her.

Joan became frustrated because she didn't understand what was going on. She was afraid that Rob was "sick." Following the principles of sex talk, Rob explained, with respect and consideration, about his early experience when he saw his mother putting stockings on. Rob told Joan, "I don't know how or why I remember that moment. I just know that from that moment on, stockings meant pleasure, love, and good feelings to me. I need them to have those feelings. Is that so wrong?" He asked her to please understand his need and to love him.

Joan felt respected, loved, and trusted. She was happy with Rob and she was determined to maintain their relationship and their love. She dropped her judgments and fears. She reminded herself of how much she loved him and that the stockings didn't really interfere with their lives together. Their love was the key to Joan's understanding. Rob was confident that Joan loved him and was therefore able to share his secret.

How can you tell the woman you love that if she doesn't wear spiked heels you cannot attain an erection? How can you share your need for a tight leather belt or long hair or large breasts? Many men live in secrecy and shame, turning themselves on with the object of their sexual connection in secret, creating huge problems, fear, and resentment. Imagine loving a woman, yet having to hide in the bathroom to perform a ritualistic, fetishistic need privately, then rushing to your partner before the erection subsides. If you were the partner, wouldn't you prefer to know and to share in the ritual? Wouldn't you prefer to be a part of the entire experience? I think most women would because there can be no true and permanent love if your partner feels shame and needs to hide his behavior. Sex talk is about honesty and respect, cooperation and compromise.

One man I know did not marry until he was forty-eight years old. He dated women with large breasts because he could not attain an erection unless her breasts were at least a D cup. Burt's fetish is his erotic connection to this particular body part. He thinks that he needs large breasts because his mother had very large breasts. He cherished the moments when he nestled against her ample chest. It was so deliciously exquisite that he relives those feelings each time he puts his face between large, warm breasts.

Burt had never fallen in love because no woman had the requisite large breasts along with the personality, looks, and intelligence he admired. The package, as he said, never seemed to come together. He was resigned to being a bachelor until he met Andrea. He fell deeply in love with her, admiring everything about her and knowing that he would be happy with her for the rest of his life. But, physically, he felt more like a brother to her, never experiencing any passion or erotic feelings. Finally, in desperation, and believing that Andrea was truly the woman of his dreams, Burt shared his fetish with her.

Andrea made it easy for him, opening the door for his confession when she told Burt that she wanted to make love to him. They had been dating for two months and he hadn't even kissed her. She was hurt and bewildered. Burt explained his fetish to her with such love and respect that she responded positively. She asked what she could do to turn him on although her breasts were small. He asked if she would be willing to have implants and she agreed.

They were married three weeks after the surgery and they made love for the first time on their wedding night. Burt's problem did not overwhelm their love because Andrea responded to her love for him, not to the oddness of his needs.

I know many women will say that they would never have surgery to please a man. I do not judge, I only know that this particular couple is extremely happy. Andrea feels completely content about her decision to please the man she loves. I also know that unless Andrea's breasts were large enough to satisfy Burt's fetish, he would not be able to respond to her physically, and their marriage and happiness would not exist.

A fetish is deeply ingrained, extremely powerful, and controlling. It is not something that can be overcome without long and intensive therapy; often unsuccessful. The important issue is communication. Talk to your partner about what your needs are, talk about what you want done and how you want it done. Surprise yourself with honesty and openness regardless of the content of your secret desire. Love really does overcome many obstacles. It is only with secrecy and dishonesty that our needs become burdens and our hearts become hardened.

Open yourself to your love partner. Talk and share and ask and comply. Whether you have a serious need that cannot be denied, or a dream, or a fantasy, or a wish, share it. Talk about it with love and respect and dignity. I think you'll find that love truly does conquer all. You can have what you want, when you want it, as you want it, and in a way that satisfies both of you. The goal is mutual respect, pleasure, joy, and fulfillment. Use sex talk to find a way to get there.

chapter 10

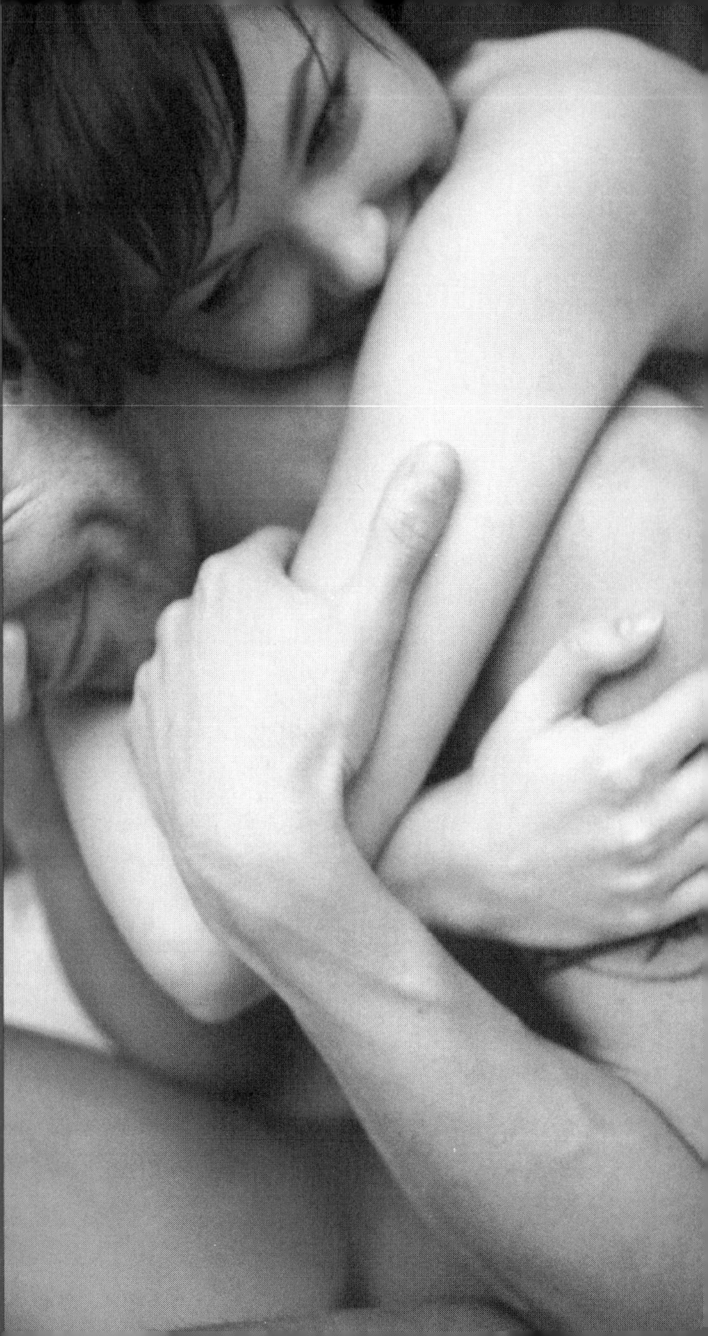

spiritual sex talk

"The great tragedy of life is not that men perish, but that they cease to love." — Somerset Maugham

The primary goal of *Sex Talk* is to offer ideas, techniques, and behaviors that will insure that you never cease to love. *Sex Talk* encourages, stimulates, and teaches you how to attain and maintain a loving and joyous life. *Sex Talk* is a guide to achieving and enhancing sexual pleasures with words of love, words of passion, and words and sounds of lust. *Sex Talk* offers the ideas and techniques that guarantee that the pleasures of the flesh are ever present in your lives.

However, regardless of the words or sounds you use, the listener has to be responsive to you. Regardless of how perfect the song of the bird may sound, you will not hear it if the windows are closed. You therefore have to create an atmosphere in which there are "open windows" so that the radiance you want to share is recognized, appreciated, and most importantly, accepted. If you hope to have an open window which allows your love to be heard and responded to, it is most beneficial if you are emotionally honest, emotionally responsive, and generously available to your partner. Nothing can happen between two people, regardless of the words, however powerful and provocative the message, if the attitude, the emotion, and the love are compromised.

We each have a filter system that precludes our hearing or accepting what is being said or done, unless we are ready, able, and willing to hear it—unless our window is open. If you are angry, or sad, or frustrated, it is difficult to accept a word of passion. If you are unfulfilled, unappreciated, or unrecognized, you are not likely to be responsive to the lure of pleasure, however skillfully it is dangled before you.

Because of this truth, *Sex Talk* offers a spiritual way of living. This is a way of life that promotes and enhances loving, warm, comfortable feelings, not threatened by a coarse and toxic atmosphere. *Sex Talk* offers a way of thinking and behaving that will create an atmosphere of sweetness and contentment. It will also create feelings that are so positive and so connective that the love you have now will thrive and expand exponentially.

Love is truly indescribable. It is an intensity of feeling, so positively powerful that no description or explanation can describe or evoke it. Love is exquisite, it is intense. Love is a life force full of warmth, joy, and ecstasy. Love makes our hearts sing, our blood sizzle, our eyes sparkle and it actually improves our physical well-being. That is truly a sign of power. Be powerful—give love.

Although millions of words have been written, there is no true explanation or description that does justice to the feelings of love. However, there are thoughts, words, and behaviors that will promote love. By incorporating these ideas you will drive the negative forces from your environment, from your thoughts, and from your hearts, leaving room only for the positive, the loving, and the joyful. It is within this atmosphere that sex talk can thrive. By creating this positive setting we live with feelings of comfort and safety. Feelings of love for each other allow us to be heard, to be responded to, and to be gratified. This may sound impossible right now, but if you begin to follow these suggestions, think these thoughts, and use these ideas, you will notice positive changes not only in yourself, but also in the people around you. We all respond to kindness, to attentiveness, and to loving behavior.

As director of the Bio Feedback Institute in New York City, I learned how powerful our minds really are. It has been proven beyond a scientific shadow of a doubt that the mind controls the body. It has been proven that the simple act of changing a word or a thought from a negative to a positive can actually improve the physiology of our bodies. If you think negatively about something, criticize someone, or become hateful in any way, your physiology will change negatively. If you change the thought from "He's so lazy," to "He's really trying," your physiological reactions to these words will be positive, rather than negative. Your blood pressure will lower, the acidity in your stomach will decrease, the tension in your muscles will decrease, your entire immune system will improve with the positive thought. On the other hand, the opposite occurs with the negative thought. Incorporate this knowledge into your everyday behavior and avoid damaging your body by negative thoughts. Begin to improve your health with positive ones. Open yourself to more love and affection, peace and contentment.

If you begin this process, you will recognize, as thousands of others have, that the more positive you are in your behavior and thoughts, the better you will feel emotionally and physically. Everyone around you will feel these good feelings. You will notice that your friends and family will be more loving to you, responding to your attitude and behavior toward them. Don't wait for "them" to extend themselves to you. Extend yourself so that everyone benefits. With such a bonus available to you, how can you not at least try to attain it?

Sex Talk strongly suggests that you accept the science of biofeedback as absolutely valid. Recognize that positive behaviors and thoughts are essential for your health and happiness. Your every thought, your every expression, your every word and behavior affects you and those around you. By changing a thought and accepting that your mind affects your body, you will experience the immediate benefits and long term results. When you speak sex talk, it will be embraced and appreciated and rewarded. There will be more love, more passion, and more joy in your life. Watch it happen.

The Institute of Happiness has conducted volumes of research regarding the state of happiness—what causes it, how we can achieve it, and what it actually is. The findings show irrefutably that the absolute most important attribute for happiness is generosity. When you are generous, it is because you feel fulfilled and complete in yourself. You have sufficient strength and joy and confidence so that you can share yourself and your feelings with others. Be generous and achieve the thrill of happiness as you share good feelings, good behaviors, and good thoughts with your loved ones.

Plato said, "The essence of man is to find a recipient for his love." This is absolutely true. If we don't have love, life is empty and without purpose. I believe that the essence and mission of mankind is to nourish and stimulate as much love within ourselves as possible, so that we overflow with love, thus inspiring others to nourish and share their love.

By following these simple ideas and techniques you will make your world go round with love, and you will create an atmosphere in which sex talk will lead to the desired effect—bells and whistles of passion, smiles of emotional happiness, and the warmth of love.

Put a Smile behind Your Eyes

Be conscious of what your expression is saying. Make your non-verbal message shine with love. Try it. Claudia began putting a smile behind her eyes and was amazed at the reaction of her colleagues. Some of them thought she'd had a haircut, others thought she had lost weight. Still others thought she was having an affair because she "looked so happy." Claudia was amazed and thrilled at the changes in her friends and family, as well as in herself.

It's really simple to do. Look in the mirror and think about a moment in which you were incredibly happy. Watch your eyes change. Watch the sparkle appear. Keep the thought and keep the sparkle. You have put a smile behind your eyes. Now, watch the wonderful reaction you'll receive.

Make Eye Contact

When you look into someone's eyes, you are saying that you are interested, you are saying you care. How many times have you said hello to someone as you walked by without looking at him or her? How often have you asked "How are you?" without even waiting for their response? Unfortunately, in our rushed, frenzied lives we do this very often. Stop. Look. Ask. Show that you really care by making eye contact. You will begin to notice that others will show that they really care about you.

Listen Attentively

In a recent research study, one hundred people were told to ask the question, "How are you?" The purpose of the study was to determine if the questioner would really *listen* to the reply. Of the one hundred people who asked the question, only eleven of them responded to the actual answer. The answer was, "Not well at all." The eleven questioners said words to the effect that they were sorry that the responder didn't feel well. Eighty-nine of the questioners gave a perfunctory answer such as, "OK," or, "Glad to hear it."

It is an absolute truth that a large majority of the time we don't listen attentively or with real interest. How many times has your spouse accused you of not listening? How many times have you said, "I didn't hear you." Make the effort to truly *listen* and you will notice that your level of intimacy will increase. An enhanced level of intimacy results in more closeness and deeper more meaningful connections. When others feel this from your attentiveness, they offer it in return. Intimacy and connection are the foundation of a loving life and a loving relationship. Listen attentively and watch the love grow from yourself to others, and from others to you.

Be Nonjudgmental

When you judge someone you are placing yourself above him or her, creating a chasm between you and essentially closing all possibility of open and honest communication. Be aware that there are many roads to travel to get to a certain point. Perhaps the road chosen by your partner or friend or child is not the road of your choice. Recognize that it might be an appropriate road nevertheless. Why judge it? Why be critical? Why close all possibility of communication and closeness? Why not allow the person to travel his own path, find his own way, and in so doing, maintain and enhance your relationship?

Of course this is not true of someone who is taking drugs, or committing crimes. But even in such situations, regardless of how sound your judgments are, they do not affect the negative behavior. Most often, to judge is to create stress and anxiety not only in yourself, but certainly in the person being judged.

Allow the lines of communication to flourish by accepting decisions and opinions of others. A nonjudgmental person is truly a friend, rather than a critic. By being a friend you can influence and actually help with much more success and effect than if you become a critic. After all, isn't the goal to be helpful to others, to show concern and assistance? Then show it with love, not by being judgmental.

Make Forgiveness a Habit

We are, each and every one of us, vulnerable and frail, needy and flawed. We make mistakes. We fail to fulfill our own goals and the expectations of others. However, luckily, most of us pick ourselves up, brush ourselves off, and start all over again. In the process, we need others around us who know how to forgive and how to accept our blunders. We do not prosper or grow when we feel anger and condemnation. We are actually pushed deeper into the abyss of failure and need under the weight of such negative reactions. Can you imagine responding to a sexual touch or a sexual word if you feel this type of negative reaction? I doubt that your body will be pulsating with passion and desire after being dealt a blow of anger and disappointment about something you've done, or *not* done. To forgive is to allow. To forgive is to not judge. To forgive is to respect and trust. See the word in this way: for-give. To give is to love. I certainly am not a proponent of forgiveness of violent or illegal behavior. I am a proponent of behavior in which we forgive the mistakes we all make. I am also a proponent of the atmosphere created when you make forgiveness a habit.

Keep Your Promises

It is a psychological truth that a broken promise causes more emotional pain than most of us realize. When a promise is made, there is a sense of expectation, a sense of excitement, a sense of pleasure for many reasons. A promise conjures these thoughts and feelings.

- The promise is of something important to me and it is made because he or she cares for me.
- The promise is to give me something that will create happiness and pleasure in my life and she or he wants me to have pleasure and happiness.
- The promise is for both of us to feel closer to each other and to enjoy something together. This means he or she truly cares about me.

You can see that a promise is not merely, "We'll go to the movies tonight." The promise has many emotional connotations. Recognize the depth of importance of the promise. Don't make a promise that cannot be kept. Recognize the extensive, far reaching damage that is done by a broken promise. Keep your promises.

Compliment

When you pay a compliment, you are paying attention. You are being kind. You are responding to something about the person that you like; something that pleases you. Put yourself in that person's shoes. How do they feel when you extend yourself in this way? You can tell how they feel by their smile. You can see how pleased they are, and you will feel just as pleased because good feelings are contagious. You create a good feeling and you reap the benefits as well.

Try to give at least ten compliments every single day. There is always something nice to notice about your child, your lover, or your colleagues. You can always comment on a new haircut, or a stylish blouse, or a sweet smile. Do *not* be disingenuous. Compliment generously and honestly. Find something you truly like and remark on it. Think of a compliment as a gift—because it is, a very precious gift. Give many gifts, give them often, and give them with love. I guarantee that this one behavioral change will make an incredible difference in your life. Each time you offer a compliment, you are taking a bit of love and not only handing it to another person, you are showing it to yourself.

Be Response-Able

When you are a loving person, and you behave with loving gestures and words, you are also aware of those around you. You notice their attitudes, their moods, and their needs. Recognize a facial expression, body language, or a tone of voice. Recognize the feeling behind it and respond to that. Being responsible is being able to respond to a need, a moment, or a situation.

Sylvia told me that she fell in love with her husband Gary when he asked her to please share with him what she was feeling. She said that she could hardly believe the words, because she didn't think that there was any manifestation of the feelings she had. She loved that he was so sensitive and aware that something was wrong, even though she had tried to hide it. He recognized her subtle signs and in so doing he gave many messages. She knew that he was sensitive to her expressions, her moods, and her needs. She knew that he cared. She knew that he wanted to be her hero, her helper, and her sounding board. She knew that he was interested.

Is there a greater symbol of love, is there greater proof of love, than to express to your partner all of these wonderful feelings? Sylvia and Gary are tuned in to each other—they notice, and they take responsibility by responding to each other's needs, however subtle they may be.

Love is truly like a light bulb. It spreads its glow throughout the surroundings, creating beauty, color, warmth, and a sense of safety. It creates a sense of comfort and familiarity. It allows us to see clearly. Love is enhanced and expanded in many ways. A loving relationship is one in which we recognize and respond.

Support. Encourage. Admire. Respect.

These are each essential to creating feelings of love. Too often we forget to tell our partners how much we admire them and what they do. We neglect to give them the respect we give to strangers. Most couples don't even say thank you, please, or excuse me. Lovers take each other for granted and neglect the common courtesies we expect from everyone else. This can create such antagonism, even anger, that they cease to be lovers.

The lack of support, encouragement, admiration, and respect are frequent visitors to our homes and our offices and our schools. It may be so subtle that we don't recognize it. It may be so unexpected that we don't even *notice* we didn't get it. It may be so out of the realm of our experience of each other that we're surprised when it does appear. Yet, we need to hear these words, we need to feel these praises and attentiveness. All of this enhances our love for each other and good feelings about ourselves.

If your partner wants to start a business, write a poem, or build a table, encourage him. Tell him you're proud that he has this goal, tell him you respect him and have faith that he *can* do it. Ask him if he wants you to help him. Be supportive. Be on his side. Be his partner. Be his friend. Be kind and generous. Do not discourage, denigrate, or criticize. Notice how much more love you'll begin to feel from him and for him.

If she wants to take a trip, make a dress, or go back to college, be on her side. Be her friend. Be the loving partner you want to be and the loving partner she needs.

Support, encouragement, admiration, and respect may seem easy and obvious, but be aware that you are probably not showing these all of the time, or even *most* of the time. Think about the atmosphere you can create when you follow this simple advice. Think of the benefits you will both reap. Think of the behavior that signifies love and manifest that behavior.

Make Your Thoughts Positive

It is incredible to see our physiological functions improve quite dramatically as we change our thoughts from negative to positive. We experience beneficial changes when we cancel a negative thought and see the situation in its most positive form.

My flight was cancelled and I was, of course, disappointed. I was looking forward to visiting my children and having some precious time with them. However, as the negative feelings raised their ugly heads, I thought about what I know to be true. I didn't want my muscles to tense or my blood pressure to rise. I didn't want to increase the acidity in my stomach or weaken my immune system. I took three deep breaths and forced myself to see the bright side of this inconvenient situation.

I would see the children a day later. I would have an extra day to finish some work. I would be able to sleep in my own bed instead of on the plane. I would help myself physically if I smiled at the airline clerk and told her I was sorry they were having so much trouble. I also told her that I hoped the other passengers would be considerate of her. I left the airport with a spring in my step and headed straight for a Chinese restaurant, since I had been craving wonton soup all day!

Remember the saying, "If you can't change it, go with the flow." Go with the flow all of the time, with everyone in your life. If you have no control, why exert yourself? If you can't make it better or different, why thrash at windmills? Accept the power you do have and change your thought patterns to positive, constructive, and healthy ones.

When faced with a flat tire, do you kick and scream and shout, "Why me?" or do you call AAA? When a dish breaks, do you scream at the person who dropped it or hold him or her in your arms offering consolation and reassurance? Never blame—it is destructive and denigrating. It has no positive or redeeming features. It accomplishes nothing other than pain and anger. Don't sweat the small stuff is probably the best advice you have ever received.

When I was diagnosed with breast cancer, I was frightened of course. But I continually reminded myself to concentrate on all of the positive aspects of my situation. I had found the small interloper very early. It was easily operable. I was absolutely curable. I wasn't in pain or restricted in any way. I felt very healthy and strong. I repeated all of these positive thoughts again and again.

After interviewing three doctors, I met the doctor of my dreams. He is sweet and kind and I trusted him implicitly. I remember skipping down the hallway laughing and happy because I was so excited to have found this wonderful doctor. For a moment I thought I must be nuts to be happy about a doctor when he was about to perform a lumpectomy on me. I changed the thought immediately and told myself how lucky I was to have met him, and even more lucky that I could see this as a joyful moment in which to celebrate.

Celebrate your life with positive thoughts. Deny the negatives by turning them to your own benefit. See the good and the glory in your life and watch your loved ones begin to see the glory in loving you and being with you. Celebrate with thought and with action.

Be Curious

You've all noticed the couple who sits in the restaurant barely looking at or saying a word to each other. The joke is, "They must be married." Isn't it sad? Why do we not have anything to say to each other? Why does research done at Penn State University confirm these words are all too often true? The study found that a couple married ten years speak to each other less than seven minutes a day. This includes "thank you" and "pass the salt."

I truly believe that we lose our curiosity about each other and about our world. Be curious. Read about a totally unfamiliar subject. Share the information. Visit a place in your own city that you've never been to. Share it. Read a book. Discuss it. Dissect the movie you go to see, discover what he thought, discover what she thought. Question each other. Be curious about your world and share what you learn. Talk to each other.

Even more essential is to be curious about each other. Pretend that you are a reporter writing an article about your spouse, or about your child, or about your parent. Ask questions: What do they need? What do they want? What moment do they remember best? What moment do they most identify with? Who are their heroes? What do they want from you? What do they need in their lives? What are their dreams and hopes? How can you help? What are they clear about? What are they confused about? What is their favorite food, shop, person, movie, book, whatever? What sets them apart? There is so much to learn and so much to explore about and with each other.

Stimulate your curiosity by asking yourself, what do you know about your partner? What do you want to share? What connections do you have and what connections can you create? How can you become closer, more intimate, more loving? Curiosity opens doors and allows you to see some of the glory and the value that you may have missed. Curiosity brings you closer together and makes your lives together more vibrantly alive, interesting, and exciting. Curiosity is a characteristic of the young and the intelligent. Curiosity is a characteristic of the aware and the inspired. Curiosity is electrifying and stimulating. Be curious.

The behaviors described here can truly change and improve your lives, inspire love, and absolutely create a more joyful and fulfilled life. It is really all about love and loving. It is all about how to find the love and perpetuate it. Adopt all or some of these ideas. Try just one for a week and see if you feel better. Try one and see if others notice a difference in you. Try two ideas and watch the changes become not only obvious, but thrilling. I guarantee you that you will be happier, healthier, and more loving. I also guarantee that everyone around you will benefit. I know because I live with these concepts, I follow them as often as I can, and I have benefited each and every day.

Mother Teresa said it beautifully, "If you want a love message to be heard, the message has to be sent out. To keep a lamp burning, we have to keep putting oil in it."

If you want love to flourish and thrive and vibrate from your soul to your loved ones, keep sharing it, keep feeling it, and keep giving it. It is only in this way that you can replenish the oil to keep the lamp burning. You will be replenishing and nourishing the love.

chapter 11

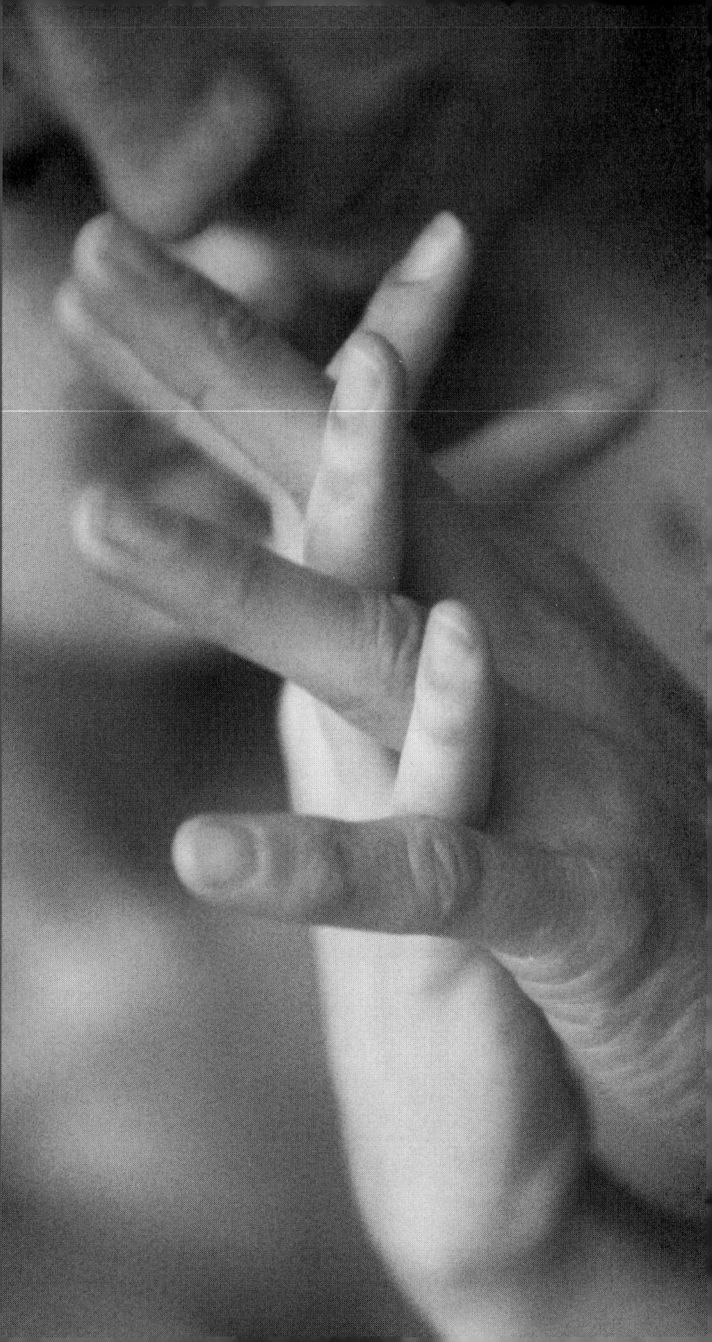

sharing emotions—what do you want & what do you need?

It is written in the Sanskrit love manual, the *Kama Sutra*: "Though a man loves a girl ever so much, he never succeeds in winning her without a great deal of talking."

The need for talking, for communication and sharing of our feelings, our needs, and our wants, is paramount for women. Not so for men. In study after study, women report that they would forego sexual release for intimacy, closeness, and emotional connection. Emotional connection is effected through words as well as actions and behaviors. Men still report that they initiate sex in the hopes of sexual release, not connection or intimacy.

Although it is true that both men and women want intimacy, very different levels are satisfactory. Women want to delve deeply and to know everything about his emotions, his successes, his feelings, and his needs. She loves to empathize and celebrate and cheer and cry for her lover's emotional state. Even though it is a roller coaster ride, she wants to take it. He, on the other hand, can truly do without the details. If he knows she loves him and that he's her hero, that's enough depth for him. He wants stability and predictability. He would prefer to avoid the valleys of emotion, and stride atop the mountain peaks of contentment.

We can see that herein lies a problem which must be overcome. The dichotomy between satisfying a woman's emotional needs and satisfying a man's needs are often insurmountable. But sex talk can tear down the barriers, overcome the impasse of variant goals, and help you and your partner merge with a profound sense of connection and love.

It is essential that we respect each other in every aspect of our lives. This respect creates an atmosphere of safety and comfort so that it is easy to share our deepest emotions. When we discuss our emotional needs and wants we hope to be understood, to be supported, and to be responded to. We hope that our feelings will be stroked and satisfied. We hope for feelings of comfort and release. We verbalize our deepest and most private emotions so that our connection is solidified and our needs are met. Sharing these feelings by talking them out is, in many ways, an absolute necessity.

But first let's look at the nonverbal techniques which are equally powerful in creating connections and bringing you closer, both emotionally and physically. The simplest, yet extremely effective, method to set an atmosphere of emotional attachment is during lovemaking.

During the heated moments of thrusting, panting, and climaxing, we are totally connected physically. Sometimes we neglect the necessary emotional connection as we become lost in the passion. As we make love we can create a powerful foundation of emotional connection. By following these simple ideas, you will weave connective threads. The closer you draw your partner towards you sexually, the closer you will become on an emotional level as well. When you do verbalize your emotional needs and wants, the bond you've woven will impact your success and fulfillment.

While making love, too many of us disconnect from the emotional realm and concentrate on the physical realm. To avoid this disconnect, try the following behaviors. These will not only enhance your sexual pleasure, they will enhance your ability to be more open and more accepted on an emotional level.

- Maintain eye contact as much as possible. There is an incredible flow of energy and love in your eyes when your body is in ecstasy. Eye contact connects your souls with love as your bodies merge with passion. As your positions change you may not be able to maintain eye contact. You are however, always able to...

- Connect with your hands and fingers. Hold hands, stroke skin, touch hair and eyes, connect in every way possible. Be aware of the skin beneath your fingers. Be aware that you are merged with another human being, the person you love. By maintaining this connection, you will be two people entwined with each other emotionally as well as physically.

- Focus on your physical feelings *and* your emotional state. It is true that at the point of orgasm, you take a flight to ecstasy and all thought, all consciousness, disappears into space. At that split second you are at disconnect. However, at all other times during your lovemaking you can remain aware and connected with love and your attention to each other.

- Tune in to the nuances of the sounds and the energy. Listen to the breathing, the sighs, and the moans. These are emotional outbursts which, when responded to, become connective strands of love and bonding. Focus and maintain this bonding.

- When you have this spiritual and intense connection during sex, it is an important step to becoming even more united emotionally. A foundation of joining both physically and emotionally creates the ease and motivation to share your emotional vulnerabilities, needs, and wants. When the union of your bodies is intensely emotional, the verbal sharing of intimate and sensitive emotions becomes much more acceptable and successful.

To Share or Not to Share

There are many couples who continue their lives in totally separate states of emotional awareness. There are others who share too much, who burden and overwhelm each other with the depths of their feelings. What you want is to learn what is appropriate and necessary and what is better left unsaid.

This is the key to sharing your emotions, needs, wants, and vulnerabilities. Before we begin to verbally share profound and sensitive issues, I believe, the following questions must be answered. In order to perpetuate honesty and essential sharing, and avoid destructive or unnecessary sharing, ask yourself the following difficult questions. If you are absolutely honest with yourself, your responses will be simple and constructive.

- Do I want to share this need, this vulnerability, this emotional statement, because it will bring *us* closer, or do I want to share it because I need to unburden myself?
- Will it help or hurt our relationship?

The choice is yours of course. Please be aware that your purpose to share is crucial to your relationship. Think twice about it if it's to unburden yourself. Think ten times about it if it may hurt the relationship. If the information will *help* the relationship, share everything, your deepest needs, your fears, your wants, all of it. Too often we make mistakes, fail to consider our purpose, and our sharing can be destructive. We need to avoid this possibility. If you feel yourself compelled to share something painful and possibly destructive, what is your reasoning? If you cannot forgive yourself for past behaviors, how can you expect anyone else to forgive you? If you know that it will be painful for the person you love, why share it? If you think or know that it will hurt the love you share, why say it?

Very often we share emotional secrets and information to "test" our lover. We do this because of our own insecurity and need to be reassured again and again. Be careful of what you share if it is a "test" of his/her love. There are many emotional issues that must and should be shared. We must also recognize the possible consequences and avoid disaster. If it's not constructive, why share?

Here is an example of a situation where sharing something difficult was the right decision: Lorie had been raped twelve years before she got married to Nate. She had not told him about the rape, on the principles I outlined above. She hadn't felt a need to unburden herself and she didn't want to share something that might be destructive to the relationship. However, she suffered from flashbacks of the horrible experience. She needed to watch her husband as they made love to reassure herself. Seeing his face helped her to stay in the moment and not relive her past horror. By holding his face in her vision she could push away the images in her mind and avoid the panic attacks that would cause her to become hysterical. She actually pushed Nate away from her several times, overtaken by the flashbacks.

Nate could not understand why Lorie would become suddenly turned off for a moment and then become loving and responsive the next. The situation was complicated by the fact that Nate wanted to make love in the dark. Since he was overweight and very uncomfortable with his body, he needed the emotional safety of darkness. This conflicted with Lorie's need to watch Nate's face during lovemaking.

Lorie realized that she needed to tell Nate what had happened twelve years before they were married. She shared her secret and explained she needed to see his face to assure herself that her flashbacks were just that. She also explained that she would suffer a panic attack and unwillingly push at him. The pushing was a reflex motion, actually pushing against the horror of the images of the rape. She was not, she told him, pushing him.

When Lorie shared why she needed to see his face in the light, Nate was very understanding and comforting. When she told him the reason for her pushing, he felt very relieved. He had been suffering from thoughts that he was a terrible lover, and even that Lorie didn't love him.

Relieved that none of these negative thoughts were true, Nate wanted to do whatever he could to relieve Lorie's pain. They compromised and began using candlelight or pink bulbs. Nate also felt so much more secure about their love, he began to lose weight and actually began to dance for Lorie, showing off his new hard body.

Lorie shared her pain with Nate because she needed him to understand the problems they were experiencing. She shared because the secret was imposing on their lovemaking and their love. The sharing was for the benefit of both of them, and it was necessary. Her response to the question was, "Yes, it's for *us*." Although it was extremely painful and difficult for Lorie, it was an absolute necessity and it did improve their relationship.

Keep these question in mind when you begin to share deep emotional vulnerabilities and needs. Do you want to share it to improve the relationship? Will it help the relationship? Will it hurt? These questions relate to the serious situations such as those discussed. If you are afraid of thunderstorms or don't drink because your father was an alcoholic, these are painful and frightening feelings, but will not affect your partner adversely. In fact, he/she will most probably empathize and be more supportive. Many couples have had horrible childhoods and feel relieved to know they can speak freely and openly about their early pains and horrors. In fact, once you share your emotional pains, your partner will be encouraged to share as well.

When you are ready to share your deepest and most private emotions, you must consider the level of your relationship. An essential factor is whether you are married, engaged, or dating. If you are not totally committed to each other—if you haven't made plans for the future with each other—sharing profound emotions is not appropriate. It is only after the engagement, once the marriage date has been set, that deep emotional issues should be shared. If you've dated a woman twice, would you want to tell her that you're a recovering alcoholic? I doubt it. If you're in love and hoping to become engaged do you want to tell your lover that you were a topless dancer when you were younger? Why would you want to share that? How would it support or improve your love? Yet, many men and women do share such personal, unnecessary, and usually destructive information.

Don't share what will hurt you and your partner. Share the building blocks—the positive, joyful, inclusive emotions. Share the emotions that need stroking and attention *if* they will not hurt the relationship. Share what is necessary for the *us*, not just the *you*.

Sharing the Tough Stuff

The following questionnaire is designed to help you and your lover share some of the more difficult things, the sharing of which will increase your intimacy and closeness. And of course, the more intimate and close you are, the more wonderful your sex life will be. As you respond to each of the following questions, remember the operative question: Will it help *us?*

First please complete the following contract. It is always a good idea to begin each emotionally charged, serious conversation with a contract.

The Sharing Contract

- We agree to complete this questionnaire as honestly and completely as we possibly can.

- We agree that if there is a question we do not want to discuss, we will skip it without judgment or negativity.
- We agree that we will respect each emotion shared and attempt to respond with empathy, support, and strength.
- We agree to trust each other to share what is constructive and necessary in order to nurture and sustain our love.
- We will share our responses and make every attempt to ask for as much information as is necessary in order to understand and to react lovingly and helpfully.

The Sharing Questionnaire

> ₁ Are you afraid of anything? Whatever it is, please share it so that I can protect you from it.

This is an interesting question for many reasons. Often we have foolish fears that we don't even think about until it smacks us in the face. My son was afraid of heights, but never shared his fear with anyone. He felt it wasn't manly to have such a fear. But he would actually become hostile about suggestions that might involve heights. If his wife wanted to go hiking, he'd say no in an angry way. If she wanted to go on a cable car he would say no. She never understood his hostile reactions to what she considered benign requests.

It was only when he shared his fear of heights that she was able to empathize and refrain from making suggestions that would upset him. Since he shared his fear, he was able to confront it and even overcome it. If a fear is restricting your experiences and causing friction in your relationships, sharing and discussing it is the beginning of conquering it. Keeping it a secret, even from yourself, is always destructive and painful.

2. Is any of my behavior upsetting to you?_____

_____

Sharing this information is a response to emotional needs and wants because too often certain behavior is upsetting, yet you are reluctant to discuss it with each other.

Betty told me she hated it when her husband asked her to drive. She didn't like to drive, she didn't want to drive, yet he frequently asked her to drive. Not wanting to hurt his feelings, or be negative, she would drive whenever he asked. But she would be irritated, and guess what? Her irritation damaged the relationship. It festered and manifested in different ways. Negativity never disappears into the night air, it drips slowly and interminably with toxic results. If there is something that bothers you, please share it and work it out. Do not allow it to grow like black mold and affect all other aspects of your relationship. What bothers you? Write it down.

3. Is there something in your past that is still bothering you? Is there something you would like me to do about it? Can I help in any way?

_____

_____

_____

4. Is there any person in *our* lives who is a problem for you? Is there some way I can help you with this?_____

_____

_____

It is not uncommon that a best friend, colleague, or sports partner is not acceptable to *both* of you. However, we are reluctant to share this discomfort because our lover is so attached to this person. The discomfort will intensify and become destructive. Share it, discuss it, and find a solution to what is bothering you about the person. Your lover will be able to help because he knows the person very well. He may be able to share something that will explain the behavior or attitude that annoys you. Or, you can find a compromise by avoiding situations that involve both of you. Having a friend outside of the relationship is not a problem as long as it doesn't interfere with *us*.

5. **Is there a person in *my* life who is a problem for you? Is there some way I can help you with this?**

_____

_____

_____

We often have trouble with relatives of the person we love. We *must* deal with these people because they are relatives. You would not respect a person who ignored a relative because *you* didn't like him or her. You would not be able to love a person who was cruel or negative to a mother or father, sister or brother. You may, however, want some solution to the situation. It is only if you share your complaints and your emotional needs in this instance that you can both find the solution.

Sidney's mother was extremely raucous in a fun-loving, partying way. Cheryl was embarrassed and upset every time they went to a public place together. She liked her mother-in-law and understood that she was more outgoing and loud than Cheryl preferred and that she was just having fun. Cheryl ignored the situation for two years and finally told Sidney that she was upset for days after they saw his mother. Sidney hadn't even noticed, since he grew up with the jokes, the imitations, and the singing. He was used to it, but Cheryl wasn't.

Miraculously, as soon as Cheryl shared her discomfort, Sidney solved the problem. He told his mother that Cheryl liked quiet, small gatherings in an elegant atmosphere. His mother got the hint and their times together were much more comfortable for Cheryl. Sidney's concern and love assuaged Cheryl's embarrassment and brought them closer than ever. Interestingly enough, Cheryl began encouraging Sidney's mother to tell a joke or two and even to sing when they were at a piano bar. In the end, their mutual honesty and respect brought Cheryl and her mother-in-law closer.

Actually, most of us need the responsiveness, the understanding, and the love Sidney showed. Often the actual solution is just frosting on the cake. In fact, there is no solution to an emotional problem. It is the listening and the empathizing that we really need and want. Often the empathy, the kind listening, the responsiveness is enough to satisfy our distress.

6. What behavior of mine annoys you?_____

_____

Please recognize that I may not be able to *stop* this behavior immediately, but I will try.

Here are some of the behaviors that may bother you that you haven't shared yet:

- You speak with food in your mouth.
- You speak while brushing your teeth.
- You blow your nose even though we're at the table.
- You chew gum.
- You leave your makeup all over the sink.
- You leave hair all over the sink after shaving.
- You never check the answering machine.
- You take food home from the restaurant, but never eat it.

And, of course, there are the traditional annoyances—leaving the top off the toothpaste tube, squeezing it from the middle, not putting the toilet seat down, etc. These foolish things are very common and often ignored. The problem is that they become more and more annoying, and the annoyance becomes more and more damaging to the relationship. What habit bothers you? Share it—you may both laugh at it, you may be able to ameliorate or even terminate it. Sharing it is always better than allowing the problem to continue.

7. Is there an activity you've stopped since our relationship began that you would love to renew?

_____

Often we stop participating in activities that don't include our partner. Although we miss those hobbies, we feel it is more important to be together as much as possible. Be very honest, is there something in which you'd like to take part again?

Peter loved ice hockey and used to play it every Sunday afternoon at the local ice rink. Since their marriage, Vera and he had been going to friends' homes, watching football, and going shopping. Peter hadn't wanted to begin skating again because it meant leaving Vera alone. They both laughed when he shared this with her because she loved to be alone sometimes, have lunch with the women, read a book, whatever. She looked forward to the three hours every week when he was out having the fun he'd missed for too long. Sharing what you need is essential if you are to think of your relationship as a nurtured and positive aspect of your life. If you feel that your love is depriving you of one of your "treasures," your resentment will build and you will both suffer.

Remember that no person can satisfy *all* of your needs. Share what you need, and fulfill yourself within the relationship and outside of the relationship. There are valid reasons and ample room for both.

8. **Are you ever sad because of what I've done or said?**
   I feel sad when you_____

9. **What can I do to amend the situation?**
   I'd like you to_____

10. **Are you ever angry because of what I've done or said?**
    I feel angry when you_____

11. **What can I do to amend the situation?**
    I'd like you to_____

12. **Do you ever feel that I don't love you? When? Why?**

I feel that you don't love me when you_____

_____

13. **What can I do to make you feel loved?**

I'd like you to_____

14. **Do you ever feel that I don't respect you? When? Why?**

I feel you don't respect me when you_____

_____

15. **What can I do to show my respect?**

I'd like you to_____

16. **Do I ever disappoint you? When? How?**

I feel disappointed when you_____

17. **What can I do to amend the situation?**
    I'd like you to_____

18. **The worst time of the day for me is_____**
    _____
    I'd like to_____

19. **The worst part of our relationship is_____**
    _____
    I'd like to_____

20. **I'm especially happy when_____**
    I'd like you to_____

21. **I often think about_____**
    You can help by_____

22. **I hate it when you_____**
    _____

One of the major complaints of couples is that they interrupt each other too frequently. There is an old joke that reflects this: "Why do you get married? You get married so that you have someone to complete your sentences."

What else bothers you? Share it and resolve it.

23. The worst part of my childhood was _____
_____

24. I hated it when my father _____
_____

25. I hated it when my mother _____
_____

These responses will be very helpful in understanding present behaviors and reactions. They will give you a great deal of information about what *not* to do and why certain things bother you now. Often, annoyances from the past repeat themselves in our partners.

$26.$ When we make love, I am emotionally_____
_____

Are you fulfilled, needy, anxious, conflicted, unaware? Take notice of how you are emotionally as well as physically. Your emotions have an intense effect on your physiological responses and thus affect the level of your pleasure.

$27.$ If you would _____ during sex, I would feel better.

What behavior, words, attitudes, are missing? What do you need to satisfy your emotional needs?

$28.$ When we're with other people, I wish you wouldn't_____

It is not unusual for couples to be loving and respectful to each other when they are alone, but to change drastically when they have an "audience." Is there something you do that is annoying or denigrating when you are with other people?

29. My emotional state is most fragile when_____

Men report that they need space and quiet time when they come home from work. They say they need to unwind. Women report they are most fragile during menstruation, or if they had an argument during the day. They need to talk about it. Herein lies a dichotomy. Waiting until he unwinds is frustrating for her. Listening to her emotional upset is aggravating for him. What is the compromise?

One couple I spoke with had a truly beautiful solution. They got into a hot tub together. Aromatic candles, soft music, and absolutely no talking until they got out of the tub. They had the candles ready, the music ready, and whoever arrived home first ran the tub. The children had grown up with this behavior and were comfortable with it. They knew it was private time for their parents and they respected it.

When are you most fragile? What do you need emotionally to ameliorate these feelings?

30. My deepest emotional need is_____

$31.$ My deepest emotional want is_____

_____

$32.$ My deepest emotional fear is_____

_____

$33.$ I am happy that we completed this questionnaire
because_____

_____

$34.$ I feel this was most helpful because_____

_____

$35.$ I love that you listened and shared with me
because_____

_____

$36.$ If I were an animal that reflected my emotions I
would be_____

_____

This is a very interesting way of characterizing your emotional state. A horse is more powerful and active than a snail. Yet a snail is less stimulated and certainly less volatile. A cow is placid, a snake is feared. What animal are you emotionally? What does this choice say about you?

37. My emotional wants and needs and vulnerabilities are yours. Please handle with care. Thank you.

chapter 12

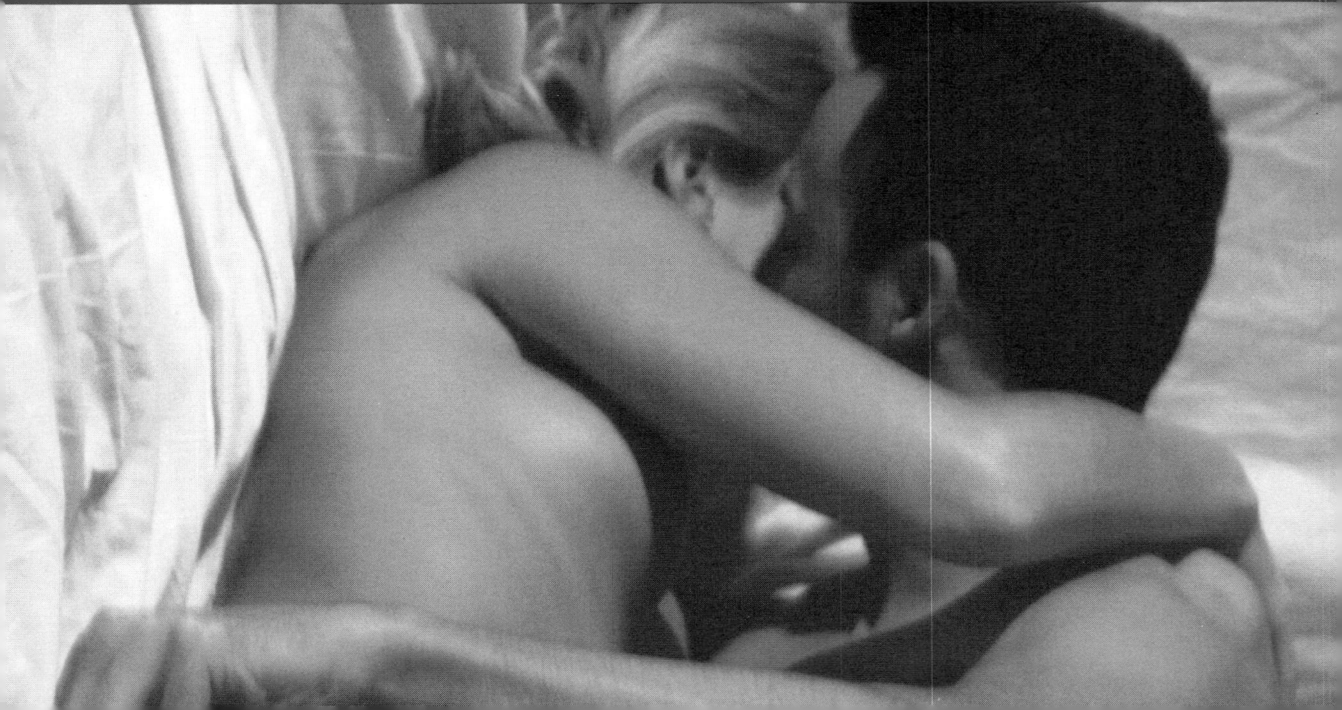

demystifying what sex should be

Sex Talk is truly a step-by-step program for the enhancement of your sexual experiences. With the appropriate approach, with respect and confidence, it is absolutely realistic that you can fulfill your sexual dreams and extraordinary passionate hopes. Be careful, however, to avoid the pitfalls of unrealistic expectations that actually diminish pleasure rather than add to it.

Too often our expectations are actually restrictive barriers to the wondrous pleasures of "ordinary" sex, "quick" sex, or even the joys of touching and kissing without expectations of wild and crazy prolonged sexual play. Realize that, while it is rewarding to pay attention to our sexual lives, ask for what we want, and plan for romantic and passionate moments, the reality of everyday, down to earth, loving experiences are often simple, quick, and too often refused because they don't fit the mold of what you think sex should be.

Under the guise of unrealistic expectations we rationalize that we need all of the bells and whistles, and in so doing, we neglect and even injure our relationship. Is the following the scenario you wait for, refusing to become involved sexually unless it is exactly like this one?

Bells are ringing and cymbals are clanging. Delightful sounds are bouncing off the walls and ceilings as bodies are pulsating in orgasmic frenzy. Your souls are enmeshed, entwined without separation or thought. Sex is the glorious, delicious, wet, and juicy delight you've always dreamed about and longed to experience. Your sex is the most transcendent and sublime of any sex you've ever imagined. You have it all and you revel in it, sink into it with all of your heart and soul and body. If it's not like this, do you say that you don't want it at all?

Is this a description of your sex life—or of *anyone's* sex life? Is this really possible, or even desirable, *all* of the time, or do such moments of intense perfection occur once in a while for some of us and rarely for most of us? I think it is most likely that the writhing and screaming, the passionate squeals and delicious orgasmic releases occur occasionally, even frequently, but not for *all* of us *all* of the time. So why do we insist on waiting, depriving, or neglecting if the sexual experience is not exactly as some books describe?

Let's face it, most advice is not specific to your life and your sexual needs. Don't deprive yourself of joyous, exciting, and satisfying sex, holding out for what you think it should be. Each and every time you join your body with your partner you form a connection, a bond of love that is indestructible, forceful, essential to your relationship. It is also true that each and every time you refuse a sexual gesture you create a drop of toxicity, a moment of corrosion, a moment of disconnection. It is not only destructive to your relationship, it is destructive to your own physiology and emotional health. Don't deprive yourself of the sex that can be yours on a regular basis, that can quench your physical and emotional sexual needs, for petty reasons.

"You didn't bring me flowers."

"You didn't kiss me hello."

"You ignored me at the party."

"We don't have enough time."

"I just did my hair."

"The children are still awake."

"I had a hard day, I'm tired."

"I have a headache."

"I'm aggravated about work."

"Why bother, what's the big deal?"

"I don't feel that you care enough."

"I'm not in a romantic mood."

"What about tomorrow?"

These are some of the remarks frequently used to avoid a few moments of pleasure. Why do men and women use these excuses to avoid the pleasures of intercourse, oral sex, touching, hugging, kissing, or merely cuddling? Why do men and women avoid the pleasures of the flesh again and again, when they would feel so much better, so much more relaxed, and so much closer to each other?

One of the reasons is that all of the above are often true. We are often tired, stressed, or worried, and we truly feel unloved and unappreciated if there are upsetting situations. These emotions are exhausting and we really don't want to exert ourselves in an all night sexual marathon, lighting the candles, and playing "Bolero," but what about something in between?

The cause of most of these excuses is that we truly believe the myth that sex should be magical each and every time. That our behavior has to be conducive to love and affection and attention all of the time. We want to feel that sex is always a communion of bodies and souls, romantic and extraordinarily connective. We want to feel our hearts beating in unison and our eyes melted to each other's souls. We avoid that which we feel is not worthy of our energy because it doesn't live up to the image we have of what it should be.

Fritz Perls is the founder of Gestalt therapy, a therapy which is founded on the now—not the why, but the what and the *now*. His disparagement of the word *should* has actually changed the lives of millions of his followers. The word *should* diminishes and negates the moment. The word *should* takes away from what you feel and want, from what you need and seek. If you think about the "should-isms" you've heard throughout your life you'll realize how foolish, even destructive they are.

Have you ever pulled away from your lover's touch because you are tired, upset, or angry? When your lover touches your shoulder in a gesture of attention and kindness, you can't allow yourself to experience the simple expression of love because you feel he *should* not have insulted you, or *should* not have forgotten your mother's birthday. You don't want the touch to turn into more touching and more feeling and eventually a sexual encounter. Therefore, you turn away from the moment, from the simple touch. What does this type of behavior do to your relationship? You feel justified because he should know that you're tired and you don't want to become sexual. He should know that you think he expects more than just a touch. But why?

You lie in bed next to each other and you put your arms around his belly, spooning your body into his. He is exhausted and he fears that you want more than warmth and closeness. He pulls away. He thinks you should know that he's tired, that he doesn't want to have sex. You think he should know that you merely want to be close. Why do we do these negative and hurtful things without even realizing the depth of the pain we are causing?

It is important to realize how much we lose when we deprive ourselves of the pleasures of touch, the romance of generosity, the loving cuddle. Romance is not the be-all and have-all that we expect; sex is not always bells and whistles. Perhaps if we recognize the love in the gesture, the look, the small attention, then we can be more accepting of each other and enjoy our sexuality more completely. Use what you are learning about sex talk to actually say, "I want to hold you." "Let's just cuddle, I know you're tired." "I love your mouth and want to kiss you even though I don't have the energy for more than that." Try saying what you mean, give the message in words rather than merely gestures that can be misconstrued. Why not say, "We don't have much time, but I still need you right now."

How often have you felt uninterested in a sexual moment? How often have you succumbed to your lover's attention "in spite" of yourself? How often have you thoroughly enjoyed the moment even though you "gave in"? Most couples tell me that if they allow themselves to let go despite their exhaustion, stress, or emotional problems, they do enjoy the release, the touching, and the loving. Most lovers do enjoy connecting to each other, yet they avoid it too often, waiting for the "right" moment, the "right" feelings, or the "right" atmosphere.

Demystify the sexual experience by making it the most natural and most frequent experience in your lives. If the children are still awake, why not have a quickie with your clothes on? Have you ever dropped your panties, leaned over, and felt the thrill of penetration for just a moment? Remember that time and how good it felt? Even though it isn't exactly the scenario described in romance novels, it felt good, didn't it? Even more important, it puts you both in a good mood, you act lovingly and kindly towards each other, and everyone benefits.

Have you ever allowed her to climb on top of you, taking you into her body, feeling your skin against hers, even though you didn't have the energy to move? Have you both enjoyed and benefited from the moment? Were you angry or loving? Were you more turned on the next time? Did you love her more because she needed your body even though you weren't ready?

Saying *no* won't take you far along the road to a rich and diverse sex life. To refuse a touch or a kiss or a hug is to follow the road to misery and anger, resentment and detachment. Why deprive yourself of the healthy release of orgasm just because you're waiting for everything to be perfect? The couple who enjoys each other on a regular basis is a couple who connects not only sexually, but emotionally and spiritually as well. The connection of sex is a most satisfying and pleasant experience, even if it's not in the most romantic setting or during the most loving time. The connection *generates* more romance and more loving.

Let's face it—sexual intercourse is a penis inside a vagina for an average of three minutes. That's it. Of course, all the loving and passion that I call moreplay, including the oral sex, the touching and kissing, the sounds and the glory of the moment, add to the pleasure. But sex doesn't have to involve candles and flowers and romance, or be wild and frenzied, or be infrequent and difficult to attain, to be glorious. So forget the myth that sexuality has to be a certain way, at a certain time, in a certain setting. Remember that saying no to any pleasure, whether limited or extraordinary, simple or elaborate, is diminishing your experience of all that life has to offer. Open yourself to the whole palette of what you can experience with each other, whether it's two hours of bells and whistles, or five minutes of fun and connection. Take it all!

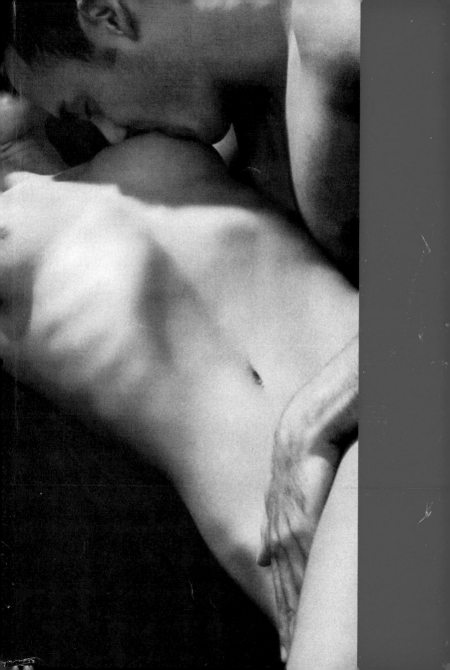

about the author

Psychologist Dr. Carole Altman is the author of *Electrify Your Sex Life*, *101 Ways to Make Love Happen*, *From the Files of a Sex Therapist*, and *Don't Have Sex Until You Read Chapter 8—Secret Strategies for Successful Dating*. She is an expert in the field of human sexuality and sex therapy, and is a popular radio and TV personality. Dr. Altman lectures and directs workshops on positive attitudes, the power of love, stress management, and joyfully passionate sex. Her website is drcarolealtman.com.

Dr. Altman lives in Las Vegas, where she loves to read, write, hike, swim, play tennis and poker, and, most of all, tries to share as much love and kindness as is possible.